100
GREATS

GLOUCESTERSHIRE
COUNTY CRICKET CLUB

GLOUCESTERSHIRE

THOUGH cricket is changing and few are
the traces
Remaining of W.G.
(Why the ball smaller?
Why the stumps taller?
Why twenty minutes for tea?),
Gloucestershire still is ' The Home of the
Graces '
To every old buffer like me.

Three was (as ever) the number of
Graces,
Gloucestershire brothers, our
Three:
E. M., the oldest,
Of fieldsmen the boldest;
G. F., the stylist was he;
And—highest in cricket for ever his place
is—
Wonderful W. G.

A tribute to the Graces.

100 GREATS

GREATS

GLOUCESTERSHIRE
COUNTY CRICKET CLUB

COMPILED BY
ANDREW HIGNELL
&
ADRIAN THOMAS

TEMPUS

First published 2002
Copyright © Andrew Hignell & Adrian Thomas, 2002

Tempus Publishing Limited
The Mill, Brimscombe Port,
Stroud, Gloucestershire, GL5 2QG

ISBN 0 7524 2416 5

TYPESETTING AND ORIGINATION BY
Tempus Publishing Limited
PRINTED IN GREAT BRITAIN BY
Midway Colour Print, Wiltshire

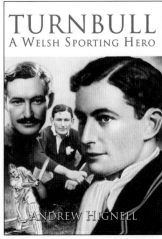

Short-listed for the Cricket Society
Book of the Year award for 2001.

Present and forthcoming cricket titles from Tempus Publishing:

0 7524 2166 2	A False Stroke of Genius: The Wayne Larkins Story	John Wallace	£12.99
0 7524 1879 3	Glamorgan CCC: 100 Greats	Andrew Hignell	£10.99
0 7524 2182 4	Glamorgan CCC: Classics	Andrew Hignell	£12.00
0 7524 1876 9	Hampshire County Cricket Club	N. Jenkinson, D. Allen & A. Renishaw	£10.99
0 7524 2188 3	Hampshire CCC: 100 Greats	N. Jenkinson, D. Allen & A. Renishaw	£12.00
0 7524 1871 8	Kent County Cricket Club	William Powell	£10.99
0 7524 1864 5	Leicestershire County Cricket Club	Dennis Lambert	£10.99
0 7524 2175 1	Leicestershire CCC: 100 Greats	Dennis Lambert	£12.00
0 7524 2167 0	Lord's: Cathedral of Cricket (hb)	Stephen Green	£25.00
0 7524 2431 9	Northamptonshire CCC: Classic Matches	Andrew Radd	£12.00
0 7524 2195 6	Northamptonshire CCC: 100 Greats	Andrew Radd	£12.00
0 7524 1585 9	Somerset County Cricket Club	Somerset Cricket Museum	£10.99
0 7524 2409 2	Somerset CCC: Classic Matches	Eddie Lawrence	£12.00
0 7524 2178 6	Somerset CCC: 100 Greats	Eddie Lawrence	£12.00
0 7524 2192 1	Sussex County Cricket Club	John Wallace	£10.99
0 7524 2421 1	Sussex CCC: 100 Greats	John Wallace	£12.00
0 7524 2184 0	Turnbull: A Welsh Sporting Hero	Andrew Hignell	£19.99
0 7524 2180 8	Warwickshire CCC: 100 Greats	Robert Brooke	£12.00
0 7524 1834 3	Worcestershire County Cricket Club	Les Hatton	£10.99
0 7524 2194 8	Worcestershire CCC: 100 Greats	Les Hatton	£12.00
0 7524 2179 4	Yorkshire CCC: 100 Greats	Mick Pope & Paul Dyson	£12.00

Acknowledgements

This book is dedicated to the late Bert Avery – another Gloucestershire Great, who died in April 2002. Bert acted as the County's scorer between 1971 and 1987, and subsequently acted as the club's statistician and museum curator. It was Bert who suggested the initial list of 100 Greats from which this selection is largely drawn, and the first-class statistics bear testament to the many long hours Bert spent, together with John Mace and Keith Gerrish, checking and collating the career records of the County's players.

Thanks should also be paid to David Foot, David Green, the late Alan Gibson, the late Grahame Parker, Stephen Chalke, Nico Craven, Graham Russell, Mark Easterbrook and Keith Ball for their rich wisdom and illuminating writing about the feats of these Gloucestershire Greats, and also to John Mace and Keith Gerrish for help with the facts and figures of these 100 players. Thanks also to the Chief Executive and administrative staff of Gloucestershire CCC, who, together with Bert Avery, gave generous assistance in the early research for this book and access to the club's archives, and also to the following for help with photographic or biographical queries – Richard Bland, Philip Bailey, David Smith, Paul McGregor, Colleen Briggs, Patrick Eager, Bill Smith, Bob Thomas, Stephen Green, the MCC librarian, and the staff at Bristol Central Library and the *Bristol Evening Post*.

Thanks also go to Stephen Chalke, Suzanna Kendall and Ken Taylor for permission to reproduce images and prints from their collections and publications. We would also like to thank 'Bomber' Wells for contributing a colourful and evocative introduction, as well as James Howarth, Kate Wiseman and Becky Gadd of Tempus Publishing for their help in the production of this book.

N.B. All the statistics are correct to the start of the 2002 English season. Figures in italics refer to one-day records, following the ACSH's list A classification.

DOUBLE GLOUCESTER.

1895 AND 1927.

⟨H⟩ADE OF W. G. GRACE (*to* HAMMOND *of his own county*). "A NOBLE CLOUT ERE MAY IS OUT."

[With a score of 192, made against Hampshire, HAMMOND equalled W. G.'s record of a thousand runs in May.]

A cartoon from *Punch* celebrating two remarkable feats by two of the greatest Greats!

Foreword

Glorious Gloucestershire – is there another county of such beauty? The stone-built cottages snuggling in the Cotswold hills. The magical villages, hidden in the ancient Forest of Dean. The mighty River Severn with its elvers. The town of Cheltenham – 'poor, pretty and proud', as my dad used to say. And my own beloved Gloucester, with its majestic cathedral and its throbbing industrial heart. The Wagon Works, Moreland's Matches, Fielding and Platt. Overlooking the city, Robinswood Hill, where we used to picnic on a Sunday. A bottle of water, a few sandwiches, and we were away and happy the whole day long. Oh, the hours we spent sliding down that hillside.

I remember how, in springtime, we used to clamber onto our bicycles and head out to Newent and the fields around Dymock Woods. What a sight we must have been at the end of the day, hordes of children pedalling home with daffodils filling our baskets and tied to our crossbars. I used to sell them for a penny a bunch.

We grew up with our own Gloucestershire Regiment, camped on Robinswood Hill. They were the only ones to have back badges – a second badge on the back of their caps, awarded for their brave rearguard action at the Battle of Alexandria. And we had our own Gloucester City Rugby Club, the cherry-and-white Elver Eaters of Kingsholm. They were all heroes to my boyish mind – but even they shrank beside the great Gloucestershire cricketers.

Wally Hammond. Surely he was the most magnificent batsman who ever walked to the wicket. My dad was always talking about his 300 on the Wagon Works ground. It would have been 400 if Nottinghamshire hadn't put every fielder on the boundary. Charlie Parker was the doyen of all left-arm bowlers. Quick, then slow. You name it, Charlie bowled it. He got Bradman twice at Bristol in 1930, and never again did the Aussie put himself down to play against Gloucestershire. Tom

Bomber Wells, standing far left, with the Gloucestershire team of 1955. The others are, from left to right, back row: Graham Wiltshire, John Mortimore, Frank McHugh, Arthur Milton, Martin Young, Peter Rochford. Front row: Sam Cook, Jack Crapp, George Emmett, George Lambert, Tom Graveney.

Goddard. He had hands as big as a bunch of bananas, and he used them to spin the ball like a top.

My father and his brothers would sit in the front room with a crate of beer, talking about them all, and I sat on the linoleum floor, soaking it all up. They would pick their best England side and the more they drank, the more Gloucestershire players would be in it. Hammond, Parker, Goddard. Before them was Gilbert Jessop, 'the Croucher'. He had been the fastest scorer of them all. If he was still there at tea, he'd have 200 to his name – and that was in the days when you had to hit the ball out of the ground for a six. Before Jessop were the Graces – Doctor W.G. and his brothers. They say that everything the great doctor did, he made look easy. Grace, Jessop, Hammond. What county could match such entertainers, such personalities? To me, a little boy in the back streets of Gloucester, they were gods. They *were* cricket.

Then one Friday evening in July 1951, almost without warning, I found myself chasing about the city on my girlfriend's bike, borrowing kit to take down to Bristol the next morning. I was to play for Gloucestershire in the County Championship, alongside the little maestro, George Emmett, and the elegant young Tom Graveney. There was Arthur Milton – what a talent! Football and cricket for England. You couldn't even get the better of him at bar billiards. Then there was Andy Wilson, the pint-sized 'keeper, and the immaculate Sam Cook.

A week later – how can I ever forget? – I arrived at the ground for my second home match. It was August Bank Holiday Saturday, we were playing Somerset and there were queues on both sides of the pavement, from the Nevil Road gates all the way to the Gloucester Road. I walked through them with my brown paper carrier bag, and I asked Bernie Bloodworth, the groundsman, 'What's going on?' He said, 'Wally's playing.'

There I was in the dressing room at Bristol, with George Emmett introducing me to my new team-mate, the idol of my childhood. What a man! He had all the physical attributes of a prize fighter. I remember Sam Cook telling me how he'd borrowed Wally's blazer and how it almost went down to his knees. I had nine wonderful years with the County. Whichever team I was on, it was always a joy. George Emmett was the greatest captain I've ever known, always on the attack. He instilled in all of us his great love of the game. We were its caretakers; it was our duty to look after it. And heaven help anyone who didn't walk when they knew they were out! The years have rolled on since I last bowled a ball on Bernie Bloodworth's sandy pitches, but the entertainment and the great names have continued.

Zaheer Abbas was a lovely stroke player – a wondrous stylist. He took chances with his shots, and I could see the memory of Hammond in his drives. Mike Procter was an attacking batsman, and an attacking bowler – an exuberant personality. He had it all. He might have been South African, but he played in the Gloucestershire tradition. Jack Russell was Mr Effervescence – a great servant to the County and a great favourite with Gloucestershire folk.

Robinswood Hill still looks down on the Wagon Works ground, but now the County plays in the shadow of Gloucester Cathedral, at the Archdeacon Meadow. When I was a boy, I used to pick bulrushes there, when it was just scrub-land, and now it maintains the tradition of County cricket here in the city of Gloucester. How many runs Hammond would have scored on its placid surface, I can't even start to imagine.

The County Ground in Bristol is no longer the open field it was in my day. It is a modern cricket stadium with all the facilities. But for the true cricket lover there can be nowhere like Cheltenham College on a Festival day – with the sun shining, Matt Windows cutting his way to a hundred and the folk around the boundary reminiscing about days gone by. They talk about Emmett and Zaheer, some even about Hammond and Parker, where once they sat and reminisced about Jessop and Grace. One day they will reminiscence about Russell and Windows.

Generation upon generation of great Gloucestershire cricketers – long may they keep coming, as long as the sun shines over the River Severn.

Bryan 'Bomber' Wells
March 2002

100 Gloucestershire Greats

Basil Allen
David Allen
Mark Alleyne
Bill Athey
Sir Derrick Bailey
Phil Bainbridge
Martyn Ball
Charles Barnett
Kim Barnett
Mike Bissex
Bernie Bloodworth
Jack Board
Brian Brain
Andy Brassington
Chris Broad
Tony Brown
Wilfred Brownlee
Arthur Bush
John Childs
Sam Cook
James Cranston
Jack Crapp
Charles Dacre
Jack Davey
George Dennett
Alf Dipper
George Emmett
Jim Foat
Tom Goddard
E.M. Grace
G.F. Grace
W.G. Grace
David Graveney
Ken Graveney

Tom Graveney
David Green
Wally Hammond
Tim Hancock
Ian Harvey
Alastair Hignell
Harry Huggins
Gilbert Jessop
Roger Knight
George Lambert
Tom Langdon
David Lawrence
Jon Lewis
Bev Lyon
Barrie Meyer
Billy Midwinter
Percy Mills
Arthur Milton
William Moberly
Cliff Monks
John Mortimore
William Neale
Ron Nicholls
Dallas Page
Arthur Paish
Charlie Parker
Grahame Parker
Mike Procter
Charles Pugh
William Pullen
Octavius Radcliffe
Fred Roberts
Douglas Robinson
Sir Foster Robinson

Peter Rochford
Paul Romaines
William Rowlands
Jack Russell
Sadiq Mohammad
Colin Scott
Cyril Sewell
David Shepherd
Reg Sinfield
David Smith
Harry Smith
Mike Smith
Jeremy Snape
Ted Spry
Javagal Srinath
Andy Stovold
Andrew Symonds
Chris Taylor
Charles Townsend
Walter Troup
Courtney Walsh
Bryan 'Bomber' Wells
Sir Phillip Williams
Andy Wilson
Graham Wiltshire
Tony Windows
Matt Windows
William Woof
Harry Wrathall
Tony Wright
Martin Young
Zaheer Abbas

The twenty who appear here in italics, occupy two pages instead of the usual one.

Basil Oliver Allen
LHB, 1932-1951

Born: 13 October 1911, Clifton, Bristol
Died: 1 May 1981, Wells, Somerset

Batting

M	I	NO	Runs	Av
285	471	20	13265	29.41

50	100	ct/st
76	14	291

Bowling

Balls	Runs	Wkts	Av	5wI	10wM
448	429	3	143.00	-	-

Best Performances
220 v Hampshire at Bournemouth, 1947
2-80 v Surrey at Bristol, 1937

Basil Allen was Gloucestershire's captain in 1947, when the County came so close to becoming County Champions, for the first time since 1877. But Allen's astute leadership produced a resurgence in 1947 as they vied with Middlesex at the top of the table. Allen's bowlers were in vintage form. With Middlesex due to visit Cheltenham during Festival Week, a wave of excited enthusiasm spread down from the Cotswolds. The Londoners arrived in Cheltenham knowing full well that the match at the College Ground was likely to determine the outcome of the Championship.

The gates were closed early on the first morning, as it seemed the entire County descended on the ground to watch Allen's men in action. Sadly, despite only being set a target of 169, it was the Middlesex spinners who held the upper hand, as Allen's men collapsed to lose the game by 68 runs.

Allen had first led the County in 1936 following Dallas Page's tragic death at the end of the previous season. He proved to be a firm, but very fair captain, displaying an imaginative and positive outlook on the game. In his six seasons in charge of the County, Gloucestershire never finished lower than tenth in the Championship.

He also selflessly stood aside in 1939 when Wally Hammond became an amateur and took over the leadership for the summer. After wartime service as a major in the Somerset Light Infantry, Allen resumed his leadership duties when Hammond retired at the end of England's tour of Australia in 1946/47. He remained the County's leader until 1950, and retired in 1951, by which time the sturdy left-hander had over 13,000 runs and 14 centuries to his credit.

Allen's highest score of 220 came against Hampshire at Bournemouth during the County's wonderful summer of 1947, and his six-hour innings was a polished display of fluent stroke-play. However, his most memorable innings for Gloucestershire came at Cheltenham in 1937, when he scored a fine 78 against Worcestershire. He shared a partnership of 269 with Wally Hammond that saw a largely unexpected victory by three wickets, on a quite spiteful wicket that was giving great assistance to the spin bowlers.

Educated at Clifton and Cambridge, Allen made his County debut in 1932 and soon established himself as a reliable left-handed batsman. He won a blue in 1933, and the following summer passed a thousand runs for the first time – a feat that he was to repeat on seven further occasions. His most productive season was 1938, when he amassed 1,785 runs, as well as holding 42 catches. Allen was a very brave fielder close in on the leg side, where he held many fine catches off the bowling of Tom Goddard. After retiring from County cricket, Allen moved to Somerset, but he still kept an interest in the affairs of Gloucestershire, and served as the County's president in 1979 and 1980.

David Arthur Allen

RHB & OB, 1953-1972

Born: 29 October 1935, Horfield, Bristol

Batting

M	I	NO	Runs	Av
349	514	110	7506	18.57
28	21	10	164	14.91

50	100	ct/st		
22	1	209		
-	-	5		

Bowling

Balls	Runs	Wkts	Av	5wI	10wM
53011	19525	882	22.13	42	7
479	261	9	29.00		

Best Performances

121* v Nottinghamshire at Trent Bridge, 1961
8-34 v Sussex at Lydney, 1969
28 v Lancashire at Bristol, 1970
4-28 v Middlesex at Bristol, 1963

Described by Sir Gary Sobers as the best off-spinner he had ever played against, David Allen was part of a long line of distinguished spinners for Gloucestershire. National Service, plus the presence of Bomber Wells and John Mortimore, restricted Allen's early appearances. But by 1959, he was a regular and he went on to win 39 Test caps and became Jim Laker's successor as England's frontline off-spinner. Allen's long fingers helped him to spin the ball sharply, and on worn wickets he was unplayable. With a fine rocking action, and subtle variations of flight and turn, Allen had a priceless ability to bowl accurately for hours, containing the finest of batsmen.

A product of Cotham Grammar School, the youngster played for Stapleton CC before joining the County's groundstaff in 1953. Later that year, the seventeen-year-old made his County debut against the Combined Services. Then, in his fourth Championship match, he took 6-13 in 12.4 overs, as Surrey chased 209 on the final afternoon at Bristol. The youngster dismissed Constable, Barrington, McIntyre, Surridge, McMahon and Loader and he was carried off the field by his friends from school.

In 1959, Allen won a regular place in the County's attack, following Bomber Wells' move to Nottinghamshire, and he finished second to Brian Statham in the national bowling averages, with 84 wickets at just under 16 apiece. Allen deservedly won his County cap, and might have won his England cap, after being chosen in the England squad for the final Test of the summer

against India. But a few days beforehand, Allen dislocated a finger in a benefit match and had to withdraw from the squad.

He won a place in the MCC tour party to the West Indies in 1959/60 as a replacement for Jim Laker. He began the tour as the least experienced spinner, but Allen showed his ability to contain the fine Caribbean batsmen, and he finished as the leading slow bowler, forming an accurate partnership with Ray Illingworth. In 1960, Allen took 8 for 41 against Yorkshire at Bradford, in addition to 5 for 29 for the Players against the Gentlemen, and was voted the Young Cricketer of the Year.

He soon became a regular in the England side, and on their winter tour to Pakistan, he returned his best figures for England, with 5-30 in the drawn Second Test against Pakistan. One of his finest performances in Test cricket was on the South African tour of 1964/65 as he bowled England to victory in the First Test.

Allen achieved the 'double' in 1961, twice passing a thousand runs. His brave batting helped to save the thrilling Test at Lord's against the 1963 West Indians. With Colin Cowdrey standing at the other end, with a broken bone above his left wrist, Allen bravely played out the final two balls from the fiery Wes Hall. After retiring, he remained involved with Gloucestershire as chairman of the committee.

Mark Wayne Alleyne
RHB & RM, 1986-present

Born: 23 May 1968, Tottenham, Middlesex

Batting

M	I	NO	Runs	Av
286	471	43	13228	30.91
340	304	61	6619	27.24

50	100	ct/st
65	19	239/3
24	4	144

Bowling

Balls	Runs	Wkts	Av	5wl	10wM
22816	11588	369	31.40	8	-
12300	9417	309	30.48		

Best Performances
256 v Northamptonshire at Northampton, 1990
6-49 v Middlesex at Lord's, 2000
134* v Leicestershire at Bristol, 1992
5-27 v Combined Universities at Bristol, 1988

Mark Alleyne can rightly claim to be the most successful captain in Gloucestershire's history. The popular all-rounder was at the helm as the club went from a position of famine to one of near feast by winning the Benson & Hedges Super Cup and NatWest Trophy in 1999, before making a clean sweep of the Benson & Hedges Cup, NatWest Trophy, and the Norwich Union National League in 2000. This was due reward for a side whose individual talents were skilfully moulded by captain Alleyne and coach John Bracewell into a most effective and close-knit playing unit with a collective spirit and keen sense of purpose.

Few could have predicted such a glittering period of success when Alleyne first arrived at the County Ground after joining the staff in the mid-1980s. Like all of the other young colts, he was full of enthusiasm and optimism, but what singled Alleyne out was a steely-keen competitive streak and single-mindedness. In subsequent years, he has retained all of these virtues, as well as his cheerful manner, and has developed into a flexible and unostentatious County captain, whose man-management skills, leadership abilities and astute understanding of the game have been recognised by the England selectors, with him leading England 'A' on tour to Bangladesh, New Zealand and the West Indies.

John Bracewell has been most fulsome in his praise of Alleyne's leadership. Whilst aware that the whole has a greater worth than the sum of the parts, the astute New Zealander believes that Alleyne's calm leadership has been the key factor behind Gloucestershire's unprecedented success in limited-overs cricket. 'Mark is a natural leader – paternal, extremely tolerant, and a fine man-manager. He has a great way with people – he works with them one-on-one, and makes them think that in his mind they are important. They like him and respect him as a man.'

It is also the mark of the man that he leads from the front when the chips are down, as in the 1999 Benson & Hedges Super Cup Final, where his 112 off 91 balls demoralised the Yorkshire attack. It also proved what a clever and inventive batsman Alleyne had become, maturely working the ball into the gaps and keeping the scoreboard ticking over to maintain pressure on the Yorkshire bowlers. It was fitting at the end of the game that Alleyne both won the Man of the Match award, and joyously lifted the club's first silverware for twenty-two years.

In the early part of his County career, Alleyne had been viewed as a 'bits and pieces' performer, but as Alleyne readily admits, this has helped his captaincy and his understanding of middle-order contributors in County cricket. Under Alleyne and Bracewell, everyone's contribution has been valued and a strong team ethic has emerged. The County took the 'art' of domestic one-day cricket to a new level, and showed just what could be

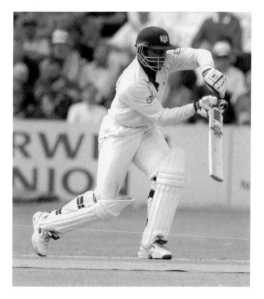

score – 134* against Leicestershire at Bristol.

In 1986/87 he was selected for the England Young Cricketers tour of Sri Lanka, and the next winter he won a place in their side to tour Australia. As his batting developed, his medium-pace bowling also became increasingly effective, and many West Country supporters predicted that the gifted all-rounder would one day gain elevation to the England senior sides. Their prognosis proved correct after Alleyne had been appointed Gloucestershire captain in 1997.

He proved to be a natural leader, and at the end of his first season at the helm *Wisden*'s correspondent praised Alleyne's 'quiet authority, tactical sense and boyish enthusiasm'. He never let the pressures of captaincy affect his game, and in 1997 he was the club's only batsman to score over a thousand runs in the County Championship. His consistency in limited-overs cricket attracted wider recognition, and in 1997 he represented England in a tournament in New Zealand.

The following winter, his leadership skills were recognised by his appointment as captain of the England team in the World Super Max 8s in Australia in late 1998. The tournament was subsequently cancelled, but in 1999/2000 he was captain of the England 'A' team to Bangladesh and New Zealand in 1999/2000, and again in the West Indies in 2000/01 as they progressed to the semi-final of the Busta International Shield.

By now, Alleyne had also won limited-overs honours with the full England side, as on 10 January 1999 he made his debut in the day-night one-day international against Australia at Brisbane. He met with little immediate success, but at the end of the tri-nations, he took 3-27 with his medium-pace bowling against Sri Lanka, and hit an unbeaten 38 against Australia.

The following winter, he played again for England in the series with South Africa and Zimbabwe. The seventh match, against South Africa at East London, saw Alleyne produce the highlight of his international career, with 53 off 68 balls and a haul of 3-55, which nearly saw England to a victory. However, a late Springboks flourish won the match in the final over.

There is no doubting that Mark Alleyne has carved a special place in Gloucestershire's history. His ascension to the heights of professional and international cricket is an inspiration to every cricket-mad youngster.

achieved by a team all pulling together, even if it did contain few players of 'star' quality.

Mark was born in London, but brought up in Barbados. He returned to England as a teenager to finish his schooling, and he then followed his elder brother, Stephen, to Haringey Cricket College, where he developed into a fine all-round cricketer under Reg Scarlett. Stephen captained the college side, and when Gloucestershire invited him for a trial, Mark went along for support. However, when other triallists failed to show up, Mark found himself playing as well, and it was he who made the greater impression. Indeed, it was his talent as a wicketkeeper that most impressed the County talent scouts. Somerset also offered him a twelve-month contract, but it was Gloucestershire who secured his services, with a three-year deal.

Alleyne duly made his first-class debut in 1986 against Kent in Gloucester and, later that season, the eighteen-year-old became the youngest player to score a century for Gloucestershire, making 116 against Sussex at Bristol in just his eighth first-class innings. It was an innings that confirmed his temperament, as he had been on 99 not out overnight, before calmly reaching the landmark the next morning. Four years later, he became the club's youngest double-centurion with a career-best 256 against Northamptonshire at Northampton, and in 1992 he made Gloucestershire's highest ever Sunday League

Charles William Jeffrey Athey
RHB & OB, 1984-1992

Born: 27 Sept. 1957, Middlesbrough, Yorks.

Batting

M	I	NO	Runs	Av
183	303	37	11383	42.79
189	185	22	6026	36.97

50	100	ct/st
60	28	186
42	5	93

Bowling

Balls	Runs	Wkts	Av	5wl	10wM
2084	1152	21	54.85	-	-
817	755	22	34.32		

Best Performances
181 v Sussex at Cheltenham, 1992
3-3 v Hampshire at Bristol, 1985
121* v Worcestershire at Moreton-in-Marsh, 1985
4-48 v Combined Universities at Bristol, 1984

Bill Athey had a productive nine-year career with Gloucestershire, during which the wiry Yorkshireman scored four centuries in succession in 1987. He rediscovered the sort of form that had led the northern press to tout his name as the next in line to Sutcliffe, Hutton and Boycott in a series of great Yorkshire openers.

In 1976, Athey had made a most impressive start to his Yorkshire career with 131 against Sussex, and in 1980 he passed a thousand runs, and was voted the Young Cricketer of the Year by the Cricket Writers' Club. 1980 also saw him play in a One-Day Test for England for the first time, as well as in the Centenary Test at Lord's.

He continued to be a consistent scorer in Championship cricket for Yorkshire – a feat made even more impressive given the growing infighting affecting the club. Athey remained on the fringe of the England team, but at the end of 1983 decided to leave and join Gloucestershire. In more peaceful surroundings at the County Ground, Athey soon recaptured his form, amassing 1,812 runs at an average of 37, including a hundred against his former club.

He continued his good form in 1985, and his consistency resulted in selection on the England 'B' tour to Sri Lanka in 1985/86, where he hit a career-best 184 at Galle. The following summer he made a fluent and accomplished 142* in the one-day inter-national against New Zealand at Old Trafford and his sharp ground fielding, especially at short mid-wicket, brought many favourable comments.

Despite a poor run in the Test series, the England selectors showed faith in Athey's steady technique and gritty determination by choosing him for the Ashes tour in 1986/87, where he and Chris Broad added 223 for the first wicket in the Second Test at Perth. Athey also came within four runs of a maiden Test hundred, and had to wait until the Lord's Test the following summer for his first – and only – Test century, with 123 against Pakistan.

Despite further opportunities on the tour to Pakistan and New Zealand in 1987/88, Athey failed to record another half-century in Test cricket. However, in one-day internationals Athey scored 111 against Australia at Brisbane in 1986/87, and he was England's top-scorer with 58 against the same opponents in their 1987 World Cup Final defeat in Calcutta.

Athey put aside these disappointments at Test level to become one of the steadiest batsmen on the County circuit. In 1989, he was appointed as Gloucestershire's captain, but the upheaval after the end of David Graveney's tenure as captain made it a difficult time to lead the club. His own form started to suffer, and at the end of the summer he wisely stood down. He returned to form in 1992, when he recorded his highest score for Gloucestershire with 181 against Sussex at Cheltenham. In 1993, Athey moved on again, to Sussex, before retiring in 1997 and becoming Worcestershire's coach. He is currently in a similar post at Dulwich College, and playing for Suffolk.

Sir Derrick Thomas Louis Bailey
RHB & RM, 1949-1952

Born: 15 August 1918, Marylebone, London

Batting

M	I	NO	Runs	Av
60	95	12	2029	24.44
50	100	ct/st		
8	2	36		

Bowling

Balls	Runs	Wkts	Av	5wI	10wM
858	388	12	32.33	-	-

Best Performances
111 v Sussex at Hove, 1951
2-19 v Somerset at Bristol, 1951

Sir Derrick Bailey was a debonair amateur who led Gloucestershire in 1951 and 1952. He would probably not have played County cricket at all had he not studied at the Royal Agricultural College at Cirencester, as it was here that he was 'spotted' by Tom Goddard in 1948.

Educated at Winchester, Sir Derrick was the son of the famous South African industrialist, Sir Abe Bailey, who had played for Transvaal. After school, he initially went into the gold-mining industry in South Africa, before joining the South African Air Force. He briefly returned to the UK on secondment to the RAF. He was later posted in the Mediterranean and won the DFC.

After the war, Bailey studied at Cirencester, and in 1948 he represented them in their annual friendly against a County XI. His solid batting impressed Tom Goddard, who persuaded him to play in a few second-team matches. Some useful innings in 1949 led to his promotion to the First XI for five Championship matches, followed by a further three in 1950 as he completed his studies.

When Basil Allen resigned Gloucestershire's captaincy at the end of 1950, it was to Bailey that the committee turned, despite the fact that he had

only appeared in a handful of games and had scored just a single half-century. The appointment of the steady, if unspectacular, batsman largely reflected the committee's wish to maintain the tradition of an amateur captain. He won the respect of the professionals with some brave innings, displaying great courage against some hostile fast bowling. Indeed, in early July he scored a maiden century, with 111 against Sussex on a lively green wicket at Hove. He was the only Gloucestershire batsman to pass fifty on the fast wicket, and in the words of *Wisden*'s correspondent 'he batted without serious fault for three and three-quarter hours, displaying special skill in strokes in front of the wicket'.

A fortnight later, he scored a second century on a different type of wicket at Rushden against Northamptonshire. This time, the ball was helping the Northants spinners, but Bailey drove powerfully, hitting 15 fours in his 101. Sir Derrick finished the season with a total of 1,003 runs, but it had not been an easy time. His team slipped from seventh in 1950 to twelfth in 1951, and Bailey could rarely lead out a full-strength side. Tom Goddard went down with severe pneumonia and pleurisy, Ken Graveney slipped a disc, and Martin Young fractured a finger.

In 1952, the side moved back up to ninth place, Sir Derrick playing some characteristically stubborn innings. However, there were some who felt that Gloucestershire should move with the times and appoint a professional captain. Eventually, a difficult situation was resolved when Sir Derrick announced that business pressures would prevent him leading the side in 1953.

Philip Bainbridge
RHB & RM, 1977-1990

Born: 16 April 1958, Sneyd Green, Stoke-on-Trent, Staffs.

Batting

M	I	NO	Runs	Av
255	420	60	12281	34.11
233	206	37	4106	24.30

50	100	ct/st
69	22	108
21	1	52

Bowling

Balls	Runs	Wkts	Av	5wI	10wM
19863	9954	273	36.46	7	-
9111	6767	244	30.21		

Best Performances
169 v Yorkshire at Cheltenham, 1988
8-53 v Somerset at Bristol, 1986
106* v Somerset at Bristol, 1986
5-22 v Middlesex at Lord's, 1987

Phil Bainbridge was an archetypal all-rounder of the modern era – very adept with bat and ball in both the long and short format of the County game, and possessing a sharp and astute cricket brain. Several inferior players have appeared recently for England, and if Gloucestershire had tasted more success, or Bainbridge had played for a more fashionable County, he might have made a few appearances in one-day internationals.

'Bains' played his early cricket for Sneyd CC in his native Staffordshire, and had trials with four Counties. Derbyshire and Northamptonshire both offered him terms, but in 1977 he joined Gloucestershire and played for Young England against Young Australia. After finishing his studies, he made his mark on the County game with 1,019 runs in 1981, plus 33 first-class wickets to win both his County cap and the Commercial Union Award for the Under-23 Batsman of the Year.

Over the next few seasons, Bainbridge developed into a phlegmatic and competitive all-rounder. His batting was neat and orthodox, and he was particularly effective off the back foot, although as his career progressed, he relied less on a whip stroke through mid-wicket. His bowling also flourished, adding a very useful leg-cutter to his armoury. Many shrewd judges believed that he could develop into an England player, and the high regard in which he was held was demonstrated by selection for the 1984/85 English Counties side to tour Zimbabwe.

For years, 'Bains' hankered after a position in the County's top order and, in the mid-1980s, he secured a regular number four spot. In 1985, he was appointed vice-captain and he rose to the challenge in positive fashion, thriving on the responsibility and scoring 1,644 runs at an average of 56.68. His total included 4 centuries and 11 fifties, and a memorable summer ended with selection as one of *Wisden*'s Five Cricketers of the Year.

Bainbridge continued to be consistent with bat and ball in 1986, and he enjoyed a memorable derby with Somerset at Bristol, taking a career-best 8-53 in the Championship fixture, followed by 106* in the Sunday League fixture. Many viewed him as Gloucestershire's next leader, but when Graveney was relieved of the captaincy, Bill Athey was appointed.

Despite being overlooked, Bainbridge continued to be a consistent all-rounder, but in 1990 he announced his retirement to concentrate on his corporate hospitality business and sports tour company. He spent a highly successful year in the Northern League with Leyland CC, before joining Graveney in the north-east to play for Durham in their inaugural Championship season in 1992.

Bainbridge resurrected his County career, and in 1994 he achieved his dream of leading a first-class County as he succeeded Graveney as Durham's captain. It was not a season to savour though, as Bainbridge suffered a total loss of form and managed only 660 runs and just 14 wickets. He stood down at the end of the summer, but was awarded a testimonial in 1996, his final year in the County game.

Martyn Charles John Ball

RHB & OB, 1988-present

Born: 26 April 1970, Bristol

Batting

M	I	NO	Runs	Av
154	237	42	3779	19.38
195	139	45	1201	12.78
50	**100**	**ct/st**		
12	-	189		
-	-	86		

Bowling

Balls	Runs	Wkts	Av	5wl	10wM
23049	10767	291	37.00	10	1
7864	5997	178	33.69		

Best Performances

71 v Nottinghamshire at Bristol, 1993
8-46 v Somerset at Taunton, 1993
51 v Sri Lanka A at Cheltenham, 1999
5-42 v Yorkshire at Cheltenham, 1999

The winter of 2001/02 saw Martyn Ball, Gloucestershire's loyal and long-serving off-spinner, suddenly elevated into the England squad for their winter tour, following Robert Croft's withdrawal from the visit to India. It was a worthy reward for the Bristol-born off-spinner, who was the country's leading slow bowler in Championship cricket in 2001, with 34 wickets at just 25 apiece.

In 1989, Ball had played for the England Under-19s against their counterparts from New Zealand, but after this received no further international recognition. Instead, he served a long apprenticeship, before being elevated to the England squad for the Indian tour, despite never having taken more than 50 wickets in a season.

At a time when there were few experienced purveyors of off-spin bowling in the English game, it was the amiable Ball who got the nod from the selectors. Although not included in Test sides, Ball proved to be a cheerful and efficient twelfth man, and spent much of the Second Test on the field as a substitute fielder, in his customary position at first slip.

Ball made his first-class debut for Gloucestershire in 1988, and has enthusiastically wheeled away with varying degrees of success. In these early years, Ball was often brought on just to give Walsh and the faster bowlers a breather, with Ball being asked to keep things tight, rather than tricking and teasing the batsmen with more flighted deliveries. His apprenticeship was therefore fairly long, and it was not until 1996 that he was awarded his County cap, largely for his loyal perseverance.

In the late 1990s, Ball emerged as a canny off-spinner, as Gloucestershire, under Mark Alleyne, became a highly successful playing unit and one of the most feared teams in one-day cricket. Ball produced many invaluable spells in the limited-overs games, drawing on his experience of keeping things tight in Championship cricket.

But Ball's contribution to Gloucestershire's success has been more than just as a defensive spinner. On many occasions, his well-flighted off-breaks tricked and teased opposing batsmen. In the West Country derby against Somerset at Taunton in 1993, Ball returned career-best match figures of 14-169. After taking six wickets in Somerset's first innings, Ball added a further eight in their second innings, as he bowled his team to a 22-run victory.

His elevation onto the international stage must also have pleased the legion of journeymen professionals who have plied their trade up and down the country. M.C.J. Ball, with a physique and stature akin to a welterweight, has kept up the fight, developing into a useful lower-order batsman and excellent slip fielder.

Indeed, his outstanding catching at first slip earned Ball plaudits, as well as the Man of the Match award in Gloucestershire's NatWest Trophy 2000 re-match against Worcestershire. Gloucestershire have had spinners who took more wickets, but few had as big a heart as Martyn Ball.

Born: 3 July 1910, Fairview, Cheltenham
Died: 28 May 1993, Stroud

Batting

M	I	NO	Runs	Av
424	700	38	21221	32.05

50	100	ct/st		
97	38	274		

Bowling

Balls	Runs	Wkts	Av	5wl	10wM
26246	11265	371	30.36	11	2

Best Performances
232 v Lancashire at Gloucester, 1937
6-17 v Essex at Clacton, 1936

Charles Barnett was a tall, free-scoring batsman whose adventurous stroke-play was feared by County bowlers and Test players alike. Indeed, legend has it that the Australian selectors even delayed choosing their team until they knew whether Barnett was in the opposition.

Some of the England Test selectors considered Barnett's batting to be too impetuous, but there was no denying the fact that his powerful batting, alongside Wally Hammond, made Barnett a very popular figure with England's cricketing public. During the course of his career, he played a series of destructive innings. Against Somerset at Bath in 1934, Barnett set about them with a barrage of savage blows. In the course of this onslaught, Barnett hit 11 sixes, and was on the verge of hitting his twelfth, when he was caught on the boundary attempting to reach two hundred.

Barnett made his Gloucestershire debut in 1927 as a sixteen-year-old at Wycliffe College. He went professional in 1929, under Charlie Parker, who helped him tighten up in defence, but encouraged him to play shots. Yet, Barnett was still quite impatient, and only recorded his maiden Championship hundred in 1933.

The turning point in his career was moving up the order in 1932 to replace Alf Dipper as the opening batsman. The partnership that he subsequently forged with Reg Sinfield added greater responsibility and discipline to his batting, without reducing his range or power of stroke-play. For the next decade, Barnett delighted the crowds by elegantly straight-driving, or nonchalantly punching a ball 'on the up' through the covers, as well as playing a fierce cut to anything loose outside the off-stump, irrespective of whether it was the first or last over of a session.

Against Worcestershire in 1933, Barnett struck a superb century before lunch as Gloucestershire raced to 196 without loss before lunch. 1933 was certainly his *annus mirabilis*, as he amassed over 2,000 runs and made his long-awaited Test debut against the West Indians at The Oval. Barnett batted at number eight, a late replacement for Hedley Verity. His accomplished 52 helped to secure him a place on the winter tour to India, where he played in three further Tests but only once opened the batting.

He eventually won a place as England's opener in the Third Test of the 1936 series against India. An aggregate of 75 runs from his bat convinced the selectors that Barnett had the temperament to open on the 1936/37 tour to Australia, and he duly won the nod ahead of Herbert Sutcliffe. Barnett revelled on the harder wickets, and recorded a career-best 259 against Queensland at Brisbane. In the Test matches, he compiled half-centuries in the opening two games of the rubber, before hitting his maiden hundred for England in the Fourth Test at Adelaide. It was not enough to prevent an English defeat, but his excellent performances on the tour secured him a regular berth in the England team for the home series with the 1937 New Zealanders and the 1938 Australians.

In the 1938 Ashes series, Barnett nearly scored a hundred before lunch in the opening Test at Trent

Bridge and by the penultimate over before the interval had reached 98. The crowd were poised to applaud his century, but at the end of the over he selflessly walked down the wicket to tell his partner Len Hutton, 'Don't think about me. Just play for lunch.' Hutton duly blocked out the final over, and Barnett finally reached his well-deserved century by hitting the first ball after the interval for four.

Barnett was a serious-minded and confident personality at the wicket, appropriately known by his colleagues as the 'Guv'nor', out of respect for how he took charge of proceedings.

During the 1930s, Barnett took on every new-ball bowler with a front-foot daring and regularly launched the Gloucestershire innings with an audacious display of hitting. His brilliant stroke-play in 1936 resulted in Barnett deservedly being one of *Wisden's* Five Cricketers of the Year as he scored over 2,000 runs during the summer, leaving bowlers despairing about where they could bowl to him. He continued in prolific form the following year, passing 2,000 runs again and recording a County best 232 against Lancashire.

When the County game resumed in 1946, he showed he was still a dashing opening batsman. In 1947 he took a well deserved and, at the time, record benefit. In the game with Leicestershire at Gloucester, he batted for over six hours and made a superb 228* – the first time he had carried his bat.

This rich vein of form resulted in Barnett returning to the Test arena, in England's middle-order, for three Tests against the 1947 South Africans, plus the First Test of the 1948 series against Australia, where he won his twentieth and final England cap. The post-war period also saw him produce some useful spells with his medium-paced bowling and clever mix of in-swing and leg-cutters. Pre-war, he had been a handy change bowler, once dismissing Don Bradman, and sometimes taking the new ball – although he later claimed that his role was to take the shine off the ball for the spinners!

Even in 1947, in the twilight of his career, he showed that he was still a fine bowler, and bowled Gloucestershire to victory over Hampshire with returns of 5-14 and 6-46. During that summer, his hurricane hitting also set up in a remarkable victory over Yorkshire, as Gloucestershire were set 389 to win in four-and-a-half hours. Barnett and Emmett made a rapid start, adding 226 in two hours, with Barnett making 141, with a six and 18 fours, and the County eventually reached their target with six wickets in hand, and forty-five minutes to spare.

At thirty-eight, Barnett was still a fine batsman and fit for the County game. But at the end of 1948, his career with Gloucestershire came to an abrupt end as he accepted a lucrative offer to play for Rochdale in the Central Lancashire League. He continued to be a prolific batsman, as well as being a patient coach of the club's younger players, and in the winter of 1953/54 he played his final representative cricket, touring India with the Commonwealth XI.

Kim John Barnett
RHB & LB/RM, 1999-present

Born: 17 July 1960, Stoke-on-Trent, Staffs.

Batting

M	I	NO	Runs	Av
40	67	5	2396	38.65
74	74	1	2147	29.41

50	100	ct/st
14	5	33
11	2	19

Bowling

Balls	Runs	Wkts	Av	5wl	10wM
339	209	2	104.50	-	-
602	481	16	30.06		

Best Performances
125 v Kent at Canterbury, 1999
2-52 v Worcestershire at Cheltenham, 1999
101 v Northamptonshire at Northampton, 2001
4-12 v Kent at Canterbury, 2001

Kim Barnett holds the unique record of having appeared in six consecutive one-day finals at Lord's. This feat was the result of his decision in 1998 to leave Derbyshire and join Gloucestershire, at the ripe old age of thirty-nine. A few cynics suggested that he was quietly seeing out his final playing years, largely at the County's expense. But Barnett's move gave him a new lease of life, and the experienced batsman was a leading light in the club's emergence as one of the best one-day teams in the country.

Barnett made an immediate impact with Gloucestershire in 1999, stabilising their top order in the limited-overs games and forming an assertive opening partnership with Tim Hancock. In the NatWest Trophy quarter-final with Glamorgan, the pair shared a opening partnership of 142 in 30 overs, whilst in the semi-final against Yorkshire, Barnett deservedly won the Man of the Match award for a mature innings of 98. Then in the final with Somerset, Barnett and Hancock set the club on the road to victory with an opening stand of 125.

Although hampered by tendonitis, Barnett had another fruitful summer in 2000, especially in the NatWest Trophy; his 86 in Gloucestershire's victory over Leicestershire bringing another Man of the Match award. He notched up 51 in the quarter-final with Northants, and hit a commanding 80 against Lancashire to steer the County to the final, and his fifth consecutive appearance in a domestic final at Lord's. The wily old campaigner is still one of the fittest men in the team, despite having played County cricket before some of the Gloucestershire squad were born. Kim Barnett was a youthful prodigy who first played Second XI cricket as a fifteen-year-old leg-spinner. He made his first-class debut for Derbyshire in 1979 and won his County cap in 1982.

The following season, he became the club's youngest-ever captain at the age of just twenty-two, and remained in the post until 1995. He developed an idiosyncratic stance, taking guard inches outside the leg-stump then shuffling into line and not flinching, despite the bowler-friendly conditions on the Derby wicket.

During his time with Derbyshire, he led them to the Benson & Hedges final in 1988, the Sunday League title in 1990, and the Benson & Hedges Cup in 1993, besides winning four Test caps for England. In 1988, he marked his Test debut against Sri Lanka at Lord's with an assured 66, and in the one-day international against the same opponents soon after, he struck 84 to win the Man of the Match award. The following summer, he made a fine 80 against Australia at Headingley, but struggled afterwards and was dropped.

It was this wealth of experience and know-how that Barnett brought to the West Country in 1999. His immediate success was no surprise to shrewd observers who viewed him as one of the lost generation of English cricketers in the 1980s.

Michael Bissex ────────────────────
RHB & SLA, 1961-1972

Born: 28 September 1944, Newbridge, Bath

Batting

M	I	NO	Runs	Av
204	343	35	6371	20.68
63	57	6	885	17.35

50	100	ct/st		
30	2	128		
-	-	14		

Bowling

Balls	Runs	Wkts	Av	5wI	10wM
14350	6491	231	28.09	11	2
343	301	10	30.10		

Best Performances
104* v Oxford University at Bristol, 1964
7-50 v Worcestershire at Cheltenham, 1971
46* v Sussex at Hove, 1971
2-7 v Glamorgan at Cardiff, 1972

Mike Bissex was a talented and ambidextrous all-round cricketer, batting right handed and bowling left-arm spin. His career, from 1961 to 1972, spanned the time when limited-overs cricket was first added to the domestic calendar. His all-round talents and positive approach to the game therefore made him ideally suited to this new form of cricket, and had he played in the past decade or two, with its greater diet of one-day games, Bissex would have had an even more illustrious County career.

Born in Bath, Bissex showed great promise as a schoolboy footballer and cricketer. His youthful prowess attracted the interest of Somerset, but George Emmett persuaded him to join Gloucestershire and he made his County debut aged sixteen against Lancashire at Cheltenham. Initially, it was Bissex's left-arm spin rather than his steady batting that won him a place in the County's side. However, he subsequently established himself in the County's middle-order during the 1960s, and as his confidence steadily grew, he also had a spell opening the batting.

At the end of 1966, Bissex was chosen for the MCC Under-25 tour of Pakistan – the equivalent of an England 'A' tour. He opened the batting at the start of the tour, and partnered Mike Brearley in the first representative match against the Pakistan Under-25 side at Lahore. Bissex made a well-composed 39, before dropping down the order for the other two 'Tests', and in the second match at Dacca, Bissex took 3-37 with his left-arm spin.

Bissex put these experiences in the sub-continent to good use for Gloucestershire in 1967. In the match against Derbyshire at Gloucester, he played a match-winning knock in the County's second innings, scoring 51 and countering the threat posed by the visiting spinners with deft footwork. Only two other batsmen passed fifty in the match. The visitors were dismissed for 96 with Bissex rounding off a fine game with 3-28. A few weeks later, Bissex was to the fore in the match with Middlesex at Bristol, claiming 4 for 31 and 5 for 66 as Gloucestershire won by three wickets.

After two lean years, he returned to form in 1970, with 104 against Kent at Cheltenham. His attractive and fluent stroke-play was rewarded by being on top of the County's Championship averages, with 1,316 runs at an average of 37, and he deservedly won his County cap.

In 1971, Bissex took 55 wickets, including a match haul of ten wickets in the victory over Nottinghamshire at Gloucester and a career-best 7 for 50 against Worcestershire at Cheltenham. However, his batting fell away in Championship cricket during 1971, although he kept his place in the County's one-day side and played in the Gillette Cup semi-final against Lancashire that ended in near darkness at Old Trafford. With low confidence, Bissex lost his place in the County team in 1972, and he left the staff.

Bernard Sydney Bloodworth
LHB & SLA/WK, 1919-1932

Born: 13 December 1893, Cheltenham
Died: 19 February 1967, Bristol

Batting

M	I	NO	Runs	Av
142	237	9	3714	16.28
50	**100**	**ct/st**		
16	1	73/28		

Bowling

Balls	Runs	Wkts	Av	5wI	10wM
91	47	0	-	-	-

Best Performance
115 v Essex at Leyton, 1925

Bernie Bloodworth's career statistics may look quite modest at first glance, but he can rightly claim a place amongst this collection of 'Glorious Glosters' for the way he selflessly devoted his life to the County club, fulfilling almost every role both on and off the field.

Bernie started playing for the Cheltenham town side as a sixteen-year-old, and in 1914 the promising young left-handed batsman and spin bowler had trials with Gloucestershire. He even acted as their twelfth man in several matches, and had high hopes that he might get taken on their staff for 1915. The outbreak of the First World War put a temporary halt to his cricketing aspirations, but in 1919 he joined the staff and made his first-class debut.

Bernie subsequently developed into a free-scoring middle-order batsman, but his liking for lusty blows often led to his downfall, and he had a reputation as someone who would go for the big shots too soon in his innings. His most productive season was 1925, when he failed by just two runs to reach a thousand, and recorded the only century of his career, 115 against Essex at Leyton.

He also acted as the County's reserve wicket-keeper to Harry Smith and, in his typically enthusiastic way, he proved to be a very capable and deft wicketkeeper. Bernie was also a fine and brave rugby forward who had played schoolboy rugby for England against Wales in 1906. He went on to lead the Cheltenham RFC pack, and became their club captain before he sustained a severe fracture of two bones in his right foot in 1930. It brought an end to his rugby-playing

career, and although he continued to play cricket for Gloucestershire in 1931 and 1932, he was never as mobile a player after the injury.

But even after announcing his retirement in 1932, Bernie remained very much part of the Gloucestershire team, acting as the County's scorer. He also acted as their baggage man, as well as being Wally Hammond's personal valet, acting without a sense of obsequiousness, instead seeing it as a privilege to look after Hammond's bats and carefully lay out his flannels before a game.

Nothing was too much trouble for Bernie, who just wanted to remain part of the Gloucestershire team, and he would relish the opportunity to be amongst them in the dressing-room during any break in play, gleefully brewing up countless mugs of tea in a big brown enamel teapot. As one colleague remembered 'Bernie became the mother and father to the team, always a soul of discretion and kindness.'

After the Second World War, Bernie continued to act as a genial and general factotum. In addition, he acted as groundsman at the County Ground, tirelessly working away under his trademark brown trilby hat until retiring in 1965. He was a highly respected, affable and loveable character, who undertook his many and varied duties with the County always showing a mix of good humour and gentleness.

Jack Henry Board
RHB & WK, 1891-1914

Born: 23 February 1867, Clifton
Died: 15 April 1924, on board *SS Kenilworth Castle* en route from South Africa

Batting

M	I	NO	Runs	Av
430	755	74	13092	19.22
50	**100**	**ct/st**		
54	8	698/318		

Bowling

Balls	Runs	Wkts	Av	5wI	10wM
22	32	0	-	-	-

Best Performance
214 v Somerset at Bristol, 1900

Jack Board was Gloucestershire's regular wicket-keeper from the early 1890s right up until the outbreak of the First World War. A fine and fearless glove-man, he was one of the country's most efficient wicketkeepers, whistling to himself as he gleefully removed the bails!

Board made his County debut in 1891, and in 1895 dismissed 75 batsmen to create a new County record. His bravery and reliability behind the stumps led to selection for the MCC tour to Australia in 1897/98, understudy to Bill Storer. The following winter, he was first-choice 'keeper on the tour led by Lord Hawke to South Africa, and in mid-February he made his England debut against South Africa at Johannesburg.

Storer returned to the England side for the Ashes series the following summer, and with Dick Lilley emerging as a fine 'keeper, Board's next representative cricket was not until 1905/06, on the MCC 26-match South Africa tour. Board played in the first two Tests, but by the Third Test at Johannesburg in mid-March, injury and illness had caught up with him. He missed taking part in what proved to be a crushing defeat for the weary English party, the South Africans winning by 243 runs.

However, he was restored to health by the time the team reached Cape Town for the final two Tests of the tour. Board even opened the batting in the first innings of the Fourth Test, and was at the crease when they won the game

by four wickets. The victory helped to restore morale after an arduous tour, but the Springboks then recorded a crushing innings victory in the last Test of the rubber. It also proved to be Board's final taste of representative cricket, but he continued to be an effervescent presence behind the timbers for Gloucestershire.

As his County career progressed, Board developed into a bold batsman. Initially, he was thought of primarily as a rather dour batsman, but he widened his range of strokes, and achieved a seasonal aggregate in excess of a thousand runs in 1900 – a feat which he repeated on five further occasions. 1900 also saw his maiden double hundred, but his finest moment with the bat came against Sussex at Hove in 1903, when he shared a partnership of 320 for the sixth wicket with Gilbert Jessop – still a record today.

He started to develop his coaching career, and for several winters before the First World War, Board travelled to coach and play in New Zealand. In 1910/11 he made his first-class debut for Hawkes Bay, and recorded scores of 134 and 195 in domestic cricket. He made his final trip to New Zealand in 1914/15 and played for Hawkes Bay until the worsening situation in Europe necessitated his return home.

After the war, Board began umpiring and in 1921 he joined the first-class list. During the winter months he secured a coaching appoint-ment in South Africa, but sadly he died of heart failure in April 1924 on board SS *Kenilworth Castle* whilst travelling home from the Cape.

Brian Maurice Brain
RHB & RFM, 1976-1981

Born: 13 September 1940, Worcester

Batting

M	I	NO	Runs	Av
110	114	27	897	10.31
100	45	16	235	8.10

50	100	ct/st
1	-	17
-	-	18

Bowling

Balls	Runs	Wkts	Av	5wl	10wM
16047	7896	316	24.98	13	1
4567	2726	144	18.93		

Best Performances
57 v Essex at Cheltenham, 1976
7-51 v Australians, Bristol, 1977
33 v Kent at Canterbury, 1978
4-28 v Kent at Gloucester, 1979

'Physically he looks like an advert for a Third World charity poster and he's not exactly a devotee of unnecessary physical exertions. He longs for a pint of lager and a fag at 6.31 and I've never known how a man who takes six months off cricket manages to keep match fit!' So wrote David Graveney in the introduction to Brian Brain's *Another Day, Another Match* – Brain's enjoyable account of the 1980 cricket season, which summed up his outlook and approach to life as a County professional aged forty.

In the book, Brain described himself, in typically modest vein, as 'a typical English County cricketer – one of 200 men who lead a strange existence throughout the apology for a summer. We get in our cars, drive a hundred miles or so, mooch around in dressing rooms, play cards when it rains, moan at the countless salads we have to eat, rub shoulders with the elite of the cricket world and then drive away to another ground. Another day, another match, and never the glamour of a Test appearance to alter the atmosphere.'

1980 was Brain's fifth summer with the West Country side, after moving from Worcestershire at the end of the 1975 season. He had first played County cricket in 1959, winning a cap in 1966, and subsequently became one of the best new ball bowlers in the County game who had not won a Test cap.

His move had raised a few eyebrows in some quarters, as some critics felt Brain was a moody presence in the Worcester dressing room, as well as being someone with a less than certain fitness record, often suffering from pulled muscles. These people had to eat their words as Brain quickly settled into the Gloucestershire dressing room and delivered the goods as a new ball bowler. Despite a few groin niggles, he proved to be largely injury-free, and in August 1976 his match return of 10-122 against Somerset at Bristol saw Gloucestershire to an innings victory over their local rivals.

Economical with the new ball, the tall seamer had a high, whippy action and a stock delivery of an out-swinger to the right-hander. But Brain also had the priceless ability to bring the ball in off the seam to trap a hapless batsman leg before. He rarely tried to bowl too quickly, relying instead on rhythm and accuracy rather than pace and hostility. Brain arrived at Gloucestershire in the twilight of his career, yet in six summers with the County, he took 316 wickets at under 25 apiece in each season, and these admirable statistics remain as a fitting testament to his skill and guile as a new-ball bowler.

He also became a key member of Gloucestershire's attack in one-day games, acting as a clever foil to the pace of Mike Procter, his new-ball partner. The grey-haired lieutenant delivered many niggardly spells in the side's successful campaign in the Benson & Hedges Cup competition in 1977, especially so in the final against Kent, where he finished with figures of 7.3-5-9-3 and came very, very close to winning the Gold Award.

Andrew James Brassington

RHB & WK, 1974-1988

Born: 9 August 1954, Bagnall, Staffs.

Batting

M	I	NO	Runs	Av
128	156	46	882	8.01
56	29	14	134	8.93

50	100	ct/st
-	-	217/48
-	-	45/11

Bowling

Balls	Runs	Wkts	Av	5wI	10wM
6	10	0	-	-	-

Best Performances

35 v Sussex at Hastings, 1982
20 v Hampshire at Bristol, 1979

Andy Brassington was another of the top-class wicketkeepers that Gloucestershire have had the habit of producing. Like goalkeepers in football, only one can play at any one time, so when Jack Russell emerged on the scene as an equally gifted 'keeper but far more effective batsman, Andy's first-team career was cut short.

He also suffered from a badly injured Achilles tendon, and after regaining fitness, he never complained at being number two. Brassington became the ideal team-man, affable and good-natured; he worked tirelessly with the Second XI, and in recognition of his loyalty and enthusiasm, the club deservedly gave him a benefit in 1988.

Alert, agile and possessing a safe pair of hands, Andy made wicket-keeping look like the easiest job in the world. He joined the Gloucestershire staff in 1973 after being spotted by Graham Wiltshire playing for Staffordshire Schoolboys in their match against Bristol Schoolboys. However, at the time he was also playing as goalkeeper for the Port Vale FC reserve team. Indeed, Andy's first sport at school had been soccer, and he did not play any cricket until going to high school, where his PE teacher, impressed by Andy's agility between the sticks, suggested that he volunteered to keep wicket for the school team. He proved to be a natural, and soon after his twelfth birthday, Andy was playing for Sneyd CC Under-18 team.

Andy made his first-class debut in 1974, and after a couple of years of combining cricket in the summer with reserve-team football for Port Vale and then Telford Town, he decided to concentrate on cricket. Initially, Andy played in Championship matches only, handing over to Andy Stovold for the one-dayers. However, in 1978, he became the regular wicketkeeper in all matches as Stovold concentrated on batting.

Brassington's unobtrusive brilliance led to his name being touted by some as a future England wicketkeeper, but he missed eight weeks after damaging his Achilles, and with the emergence of Jack Russell in the early 1980s, a Test career was not to be. Ironically, Andy had been one of the first members of the County's staff to coach the schoolboy Russell during winter nets at Bristol. As Jack later recalled, 'his coaching was brilliant, and after I saw him play for the first time against the West Indies at Bristol in 1980, I modelled myself on his technique. Purely and simply for the fact that he was superb.'

He accepted the role as reserve 'keeper with good grace, and continued to play for the second team and, occasionally, the First XI with the same enthusiasm that he had done as a youngster. He retired from playing in 1988, and subsequently moved into the club's marketing department, with his happy, ever-smiling face being one of the integral features at the Nevil Road ground. He has subsequently taken a similar post with Bristol RFC.

Brian Christopher Broad

LHB & RM, 1979-1994

Born: 29 September 1957, Knowle

Batting

M	I	NO	Runs	Av
118	215	9	6549	31.79
92	89	4	2435	28.65

50	100	ct/st
31	11	50
13	1	24

Bowling

Balls	Runs	Wkts	Av	5wl	10wM
1128	657	11	59.72	-	-
813	712	19	37.47		

Best Performances

145 v Nottinghamshire at Bristol, 1983
2-14 v West Indians at Bristol, 1980
114* v Yorkshire at Bristol, 1992
3-46 v Worcestershire at Bristol, 1982

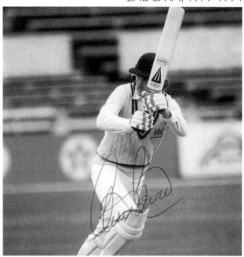

Chris Broad had two spells with Gloucestershire from 1979 until 1994, punctuated by time with Nottinghamshire between 1984 and 1992, after the tall, opening batsman left his native Bristol in a quest to win a Test cap with England.

The former Colston schoolboy won a regular place in the Gloucestershire side in 1980, and soon established himself as a fluent stroke-player. Broad was very ambitious with a single-mindedness of purpose, and towards the end of 1983 he stated his desire to play Test cricket. In passing, he also made slighting reference to some of his Gloucestershire colleagues, and gave the impression that he was disillusioned with life at Nevil Road and that this was stifling his ambitions.

Permission for the interview had not been sought, but the club decided not to seek punitive action, and instead permitted Broad to leave the club. He duly joined Nottinghamshire for 1984, and only a few weeks after making his debut for the club, he was drafted into the England side for the Second Test of the series with the West Indies. He marked his England debut with a typically assured 55 and never flinched against the illustrious Caribbean fast bowlers. Broad's swift elevation into the England side was based on his reputation as one of the best players in the country against quick bowling. He was strong off the back foot, utilising his tall frame and upright stance at the crease, with

his most productive shot being a solid clip off his legs through mid-wicket. Of his contemporaries, only Graham Gooch was better against pace.

On the 1986/87 tour to Australia, Broad confirmed his abilities on quick wickets with 162 in the Second Test at Perth, 116 in the Third Test at Adelaide and 112 in the Fourth Test at Melbourne. He was just the fourth Englishman – after Hobbs, Hammond and Woolmer – to score hundreds in three successive Ashes Tests.

Following this superb tour, it looked as if Broad would become a permanent fixture in the England side, but the following winter he had a particularly unhappy tour of Pakistan, where he suffered from several poor umpiring decisions. Even though he scored a century at Faisalabad, Broad met with censure after almost refusing to leave the crease when given out in Lahore.

A month later, Broad met with further controversy as he smashed down his stumps in the Bicentenary Test at Sydney, and it was this show of petulance, rather than a fine hundred, that remained in the minds of England's hierarchy.

Broad had a fine summer in 1990, amassing 2,226 runs (average 54), cashing in on the grass-less pitches and low-seamed balls as bowlers up and down the country wilted under a veritable deluge of runs from all of the country's leading batsmen. In 1993 he returned to Gloucestershire, but during his second season 'back home' he began to be affected by an arthritic hip. The following summer, this forced Broad into retirement, and he subsequently pursued a career in sport on radio and television.

Anthony Stephen Brown
RHB & RM, 1953-1976

Born: 24 June 1936, Clifton

Batting

M	I	NO	Runs	Av
489	797	98	1281	18.14
160	140	27	2011	17.80

50	100	ct/st		
40	3	488		
2	-	68		

Bowling

Balls	Runs	Wkts	Av	5wI	10wM
70876	31159	1223	25.47	54	8
7530	4684	228	20.54		

Best Performances
116 v Somerset at Bristol, 1971
8-80 v Essex at Leyton, 1963
77* v Sussex at Lord's, 1973
5-44 v Derbyshire at Chesterfield, 1975

Tony Brown was Gloucestershire's captain and the Man of the Match in the 1973 Gillette Cup final. He rose to the occasion with an astute unbroken innings of 77 that ensured his side set Sussex a sizeable target. However, a different outcome had seemed likely when Brown came to the wicket with the scoreboard reading Gloucestershire 106-5, but the experienced all-rounder was undeterred and after useful partnerships with Mike Procter and Jim Foat, Brown was able to guide his side to a total of 248-8.

During the last eight overs, Brown gave a fine display of controlled aggression, twice hoisting Tony Greig for huge sixes over the long leg and square leg boundary. When Gloucestershire fielded, Brown adroitly marshalled his troops, made some perceptive bowling changes and delivered twelve overs of accurate seam bowling to thwart Sussex's ambitions. When Sussex ended 40 runs short, there was only one real candidate for Man of the Match – A.S. Brown.

Brown had joined the County's staff primarily as a batsman who bowled occasionally, and in early July 1953, he made his first-class debut, batting in the middle-order against Yorkshire at Sheffield, a month after his seventeenth birthday. Brown's father had been a Welsh schoolboy soccer international, and young Tony also showed promise at both soccer and rugby, winning a place in the Bristol Public Schools rugby team, as well as playing at centre-forward

for the Gloucestershire Amateurs football side, and winning a trial with Newport County.

After leaving school and doing his National Service, Brown gained a regular place in the Gloucestershire side in 1957 as David Smith's partner with the new ball. He extracted a lively pace from his relatively short run, fully utilising his lithe and easy-flowing action. In addition, he showed great control of swing and movement off the pitch, and had a faster ball that surprised many experienced opponents. At the end of the 1957 season, George Emmett awarded the young all-rounder his County cap, saying 'This is not for what you have done for Gloucestershire, but for what I know you will do in the future.'

Brown soon proved him right, and during 1959 Brown took over 100 wickets. The highlight was 7-11 against Yorkshire at Bristol during August, as the side that eventually won the Championship experienced a rare off-day, and were bustled out for 35 as Gloucestershire recorded an innings victory.

During the early 1960s, Brown continued to form a fine new-ball partnership alongside David Smith, with Brown taking over a hundred wickets in 1962, and taking a career-best 8-80 in the first innings of the match against Essex at Leyton in 1963. Brown's swing and pace accounted for the first six wickets at a cost of just

19 runs as Essex slumped to 43-6, before some lusty blows by the Essex tail dented Brown's figures and saw Essex recover to a more healthy position. Essex eventually snatched victory in the final hour of the third day.

Brown also developed into a fine fielder close to the wicket, and in 1966, during Nottinghamshire's second innings of the match at Trent Bridge, he equalled the world record of seven catches in an innings, set by Surrey's Micky Stewart in 1957. His feat came as the home team batted on a damp wicket, with the ball lifting alarmingly. But, as Tony modestly recalled, 'my first was a caught and bowled. I did have to dive for that one, but the other six were taken close to the wicket – at slip off David Smith, short leg and gully to left and right-handers off Mike Bissex and David Allen. In every case, the ball lifted and carried five or six yards straight to me at a comfortable height!'

In 1969, Brown took over the County captaincy. It had been a period of modest success for the West Country side. In the preceding five years, they had twice been at the bottom of the County table, as well as next to last on another occasion. With great drive and initiative, Brown turned things around dramatically, as Gloucestershire finished runners-up in his first season in charge and were then third in 1970. Their progress was an indication of Brown's shrewd captaincy, and he helped forge a Gloucestershire side effective at both the longer form of the game, as well as in limited-over games. Their triumph in the Gillette Cup final in 1973 was a culmination of his aggressive philosophy of always looking to bowl opponents out, rather than contain them and wait for a batsman to falter.

His time in charge also coincided with the emergence of Mike Procter as a world-class all-rounder. This added an extra dimension to the Gloucestershire attack and eased the burden on Brown's shoulders. It also allowed him to become a clever change bowler, taking a hat-trick against Glamorgan at Swansea in 1973, as well as still being an effective middle-order batsman, recording a career-best 116 against Somerset at Bristol in 1971.

At the end of the season, Brown also took on various roles off the field as the club tried to reduce its sizeable overdraft. The committee felt

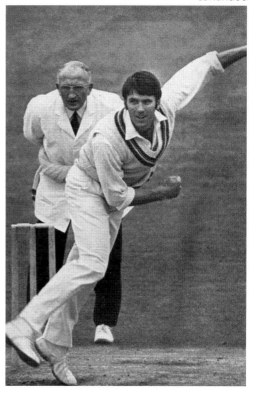

that there was a need for fresh ideas, so Brown became the County's assistant secretary, with specific responsibilities for public relations, advertising and the creation of a target golf range to bring in extra capital during the winter months. Brown proved to be a capable administrator, and in 1976 he took over as the club's secretary/manager. This administrative reshuffle prompted his retirement from the County game, and he continued in this role until 1982, when he moved to Somerset to fulfil a similar role.

He remained with Somerset for the next six years, during which time his managerial skills became increasingly recognised by Lord's. He acted as manager of England's tour to Sri Lanka, India and Australia in 1984/85 and to the West Indies in 1985/86 – both with David Gower as captain – and at the end of the 1988 season was appointed assistant secretary of the Test and County Cricket Board. He remained at Lord's until retiring in 1997, and in his final year at the game's headquarters he was administration manager of the newly-formed England and Wales Cricket Board.

Born: 18 April 1890, Cotham, Redland, Bristol
Died: 12 October 1914, Wyke Regis, Dorset

Batting

M	I	NO	Runs	Av
32	51	4	764	16.25
50	100	ct/st		
3	-	25		

Bowling

Balls	Runs	Wkts	Av	5wI	10wM
1987	1173	40	29.32	2	-

Best Performances
68 v Northamptonshire at Bristol, 1910
6-84 v Worcestershire at Cheltenham, 1910

Wilfred Brownlee was a gifted schoolboy cricketer and racquets player at Clifton College, and in 1909 he followed his older brother into the Gloucestershire XI. Despite morale within the County being at low ebb, he made an immediate impact, and looked like becoming a fine all-rounder. Tragically, the twenty-four-year-old player died early in the the First World War – the loss of a potentially great name in the club's history.

Brownlee was born into a real cricketing family, with his father, Methven, being W.G. Grace's biographer, whilst elder brother Leigh won a blue at Oxford in 1904 and a place in the Gloucestershire side from 1901. Wilfred played in the Clifton side from 1906, during which time, his wristy stroke-play, fast medium swing bowler, and athletic fielding marked him out as a young cricketer of exceptional promise. Some felt that he was the college's finest all-rounder since Charles Townsend, whilst in 1909 *Wisden's* correspondent wrote that 'in Brownlee, Clifton have produced a cricketer of class, a brilliant fielder, good bowler and stylish batsman'.

Brownlee captained the Clifton XI in 1909 with great distinction, and his outstanding efforts led to selection in August for the Public Schools against the MCC at Lord's. Brownlee had a fine match with the ball, returning figures of 8-61 as the Public Schools won by two wickets, with Brownlee deceiving the MCC side with late swerve and swing.

The previous week at Worcester, Brownlee had made his Gloucestershire debut, and he soon impressed with the bat, finishing the game as the County's top scorer after playing a mature innings of 64. The youngster's efforts nearly led to Gloucestershire victory, but amidst growing excitement, Worcestershire got home with a narrow one-wicket victory.

Brownlee played in five further games for Gloucestershire in August 1909, and his bold and free hitting in the middle order helped to lift the County's morale during what had become quite a poor season. In the match with Essex at Cheltenham, the youngster delighted the Festival crowd by sharing a quick-fire partnership with Tom Langdon, in which the pair, in the space of just twenty-five minutes, added 91 in only 10 overs, as Gloucestershire strove hard to press for victory in a rain-ravaged contest.

In 1912, Brownlee went to Corpus Christi, Cambridge, and was only available for the County during his summer vacations. Even so, he played several cameos with the bat and also started to show that he could develop into a very useful swing bowler at County level.

Many Gloucestershire supporters hoped that the gifted amateur would fairly soon be able to establish a regular place in the County eleven, but the onset of the First World War intervened, as Brownlee joined the 3rd Dorset Regiment. Sadly, he contracted meningitis, and died on 12 October 1914.

James Arthur Bush
LHB & WK, 1870-1890

Born: 28 July 1850, Cawnpore, India
Died: 21 September 1924, Clevedon, Somerset

Batting

M	I	NO	Runs	Av
136	207	61	1186	8.12
50	100	ct/st		
2	-	186/81		

Bowling

Balls	Runs	Wkts	Av	5wI	10wM
136	65	0	-	-	-

Best Performances
57 v Yorkshire at Sheffield, 1879

'Frizzie' Bush was the first in a long line of great Gloucestershire's wicketkeepers, excelling behind the stumps during their golden era of the 1870s. The Old Cliftonian was one of the closest friends of W.G. Grace, and on 9 October 1873 Bush acted as best man at the doctor's wedding in London. The be-whiskered Bush made his Gloucestershire debut in 1870, initially as a batsman, before trying his chances behind the stumps. He had kept wicket as a schoolboy at Clifton, and 'Frizzie' soon won a regular place as the County's 'keeper, performing with great skill.

By the mid-1870s, Bush was regarded as the finest amateur wicketkeeper in the country, playing in 1874 and 1875 for the Gentlemen against the Players at Lord's and touring Australia with Grace's XI in 1873/74. However, his finest moment for the Gentlemen came in 1878, when he helped defeat the Australians at Prince's by an innings and one run.

In addition to having a very safe pair of hands, Bush was a steady batsman and someone who could be relied upon to play a defensive innings. In 1876 against Yorkshire at Cheltenham, the wicketkeeper adopted the role of sheet anchor as W.G. became the first Gloucestershire batsman to score a triple hundred. The doctor was several runs short of 300 when Bush made his way to the wicket. 'Don't worry', he told his good friend, 'I'll stay here until you get your runs.' By the time Bush was dismissed for 32, W.G. had moved on to 318* and his score was to remain the highest in a County match for the next twenty years.

A notoriously bad starter with the bat, he was bowled by the first ball of an exhibition match at Kadina on the Australian tour of 1873/74. But rather than turning to walk back to the pavilion, 'Frizzie' calmly bent down and put the bails back on the stumps, saying to the local umpire, 'I never could play a trial ball, and I wish the cricket authorities would expunge it from the rules.' Believing this to be correct, the local man nodded in agreement, waved dead ball to the scorers, and Bush continued his innings.

Born in India, Bush hailed from a military family, with his father serving as the commanding officer of the Bristol Rifles. He had also been an outstanding schoolboy sportsman at Clifton, winning honours at cricket and rugby, and in February 1872 he became the first Gloucestershire man to win an English rugby cap, playing for England against Scotland at The Oval. He went on to add a further four caps in an illustrious career with Clifton RFC.

From the 1880s, Bush also gave over twenty years of service on Gloucestershire's cricket committee. In 1884, he was one of the sub-committee that oversaw purchase of land at Ashley Down, at which the County subsequently developed headquarters. Later in 1899, he tried to persuade W.G. to remain with the County side, but after many long nights spent talking and drinking, the doctor severed his connection with the County side.

Born: 15 August 1951, Plymouth, Devon

Batting

M	I	NO	Runs	Av
165	151	72	535	6.77
74	29	18	121	11.00
50	**100**	**ct/st**		
-	-	63		
-	-	12		

Bowling

Balls	Runs	Wkts	Av	5wI	10wM
29800	13468	421	31.99	21	2
3205	2090	60	34.83		

Best Performances
34* v Nottinghamshire at Cheltenham, 1982
9-56 v Somerset at Bristol, 1981
16 v Nottinghamshire at Trent Bridge, 1981*
4-15 v Northamptonshire at Northampton, 1976

In 1988, John Childs made his Test debut at the ripe old age of 36 years and 320 days – England's oldest debutant for forty years. It was a quite remarkable turnaround in the career of the cheerful, left-arm orthodox spinner, who had enjoyed a steady ten-year career with Gloucestershire, largely in the shadow of David Graveney, only to lose his form, confidence and place, both in the West Country team and on their staff in 1984.

He subsequently remodelled his action, seeking advice from Fred Titmus and Don Wilson at the MCC Indoor School; he wrote letters to every County bar Yorkshire to see if he might secure a contract for the following summer. Eventually, Essex offered him a one-year contract for 1985, but Childs only took five wickets at a cost of 105 runs apiece, and it seemed his professional career was over.

However, Essex offered him terms for the following summer, and he spent the winter of 1985/86 working as a freelance sign-writer and undergoing further remedial work with the coaches at Lord's, developing a straighter, longer and faster approach to the wicket. Childs put this valuable advice and practice to good use in 1986, as he made a remarkable return to form, with 89 wickets as Essex won the County Championship, and he became one of *Wisden*'s Five Cricketers of the Year.

He enjoyed another vintage season in 1987, and by 1988 was regarded as the country's leading left-arm spinner. Childs made his Test debut against the West Indians in the Third Test of their 1988 series at Old Trafford, and added a second cap at The Oval in the Fifth Test. Even though both ended in defeat, Childs remained in the thoughts of the selectors, and was in the MCC party for the winter tour to India. However, the tour was cancelled when the Indian government objected to the links several players had with South Africa. Despite being included in the squad for the Headingley Test of 1992, he was not called up again.

'Charlie' Childs was brought up in the Torquay area, and progressed from village cricket with Kingskerwell into the Devon youth teams, and eventually their Minor County side. In 1974, he impressed Gloucestershire coach Graham Wiltshire whilst playing for Devon against Cornwall. The Devonian's left-arm spin and old-fashioned craft eventually led to a contract.

Childs made his Gloucestershire debut in 1975 and the following year he enjoyed a fine time at the Cheltenham Festival, taking 8-71 against Essex. In 1977, he won his County cap, and formed an effective spin partnership with David Graveney, with the pair claiming 105 wickets between them. In 1981, Childs enjoyed his best summer for Gloucestershire with 75 wickets.

Born: 23 August 1921, Tetbury
Died: 4 September 1996, Tetbury

Batting

M	I	NO	Runs	Av
498	601	244	1936	5.42
50	100	ct/st		
-	-	148		

Bowling

Balls	Runs	Wkts	Av	5wI	10wM
105183	35929	1768	20.32	98	15

Best Performances
35* v Sussex at Hove, 1957
9-42 v Yorkshire at Bristol, 1947

Sam Cook was the epitome of a West Country cricketer. A loyal and phlegmatic character with a warm and wry sense of humour, he gave Gloucestershire nineteen years of sterling service as a left-arm spinner. During this time, the 'Tetbury Twirler' took 1,768 wickets in first-class cricket, after achieving the feat of a wicket with his first ever ball in County cricket, against Oxford University in 1946.

Given his fine County record, Sam could consider himself unlucky to have won a solitary Test cap, against the 1947 South Africans. To an extent, he was unlucky to have been a contemporary of Jack Young, Johnny Wardle and later, Tony Lock. But Sam was a very down-to-earth person, never giving himself any airs and graces, or moaning about his misfortune. In fact, the acclaim of winning a Test cap rather embarrassed Sam, and he was perfectly content with his life on the County circuit, taking a regular bag of wickets for his native Gloucestershire and then sitting down quietly after play to savour a pint or two.

On leaving school, Cook trained as a plumber, never thinking that he was remotely good enough to be a professional cricketer. However, whilst serving with the RAF, Sam was posted to the Flying Training School in Bulawayo and he got the inkling that he might, after all, be good enough to become a County cricketer. Before the war, he had been successful for the Tetbury side as a spin bowler, and he met with further success in Forces cricket, besides scoring two hundreds in rather unconven-

tional style. It was Sam's accurate bowling that impressed his RAF captain, Sandy Singleton, the Worcestershire amateur, and after some fine performances, Sandy suggested that Sam should have a trial with Gloucestershire.

When the hostilities were over, Sam followed Singleton's recommendations and in the spring of 1946 he travelled to the Nevil Road ground. He arrived at the nets at Bristol, knowing few of the County's players, and walked over to Wally Hammond, introducing himself as 'Cook of Tetbury, Sir'. Hammond was soon impressed by the way the virtually unknown spinner quickly hit a perfect length, and caused the more experienced batsmen to play and miss. With a smile on his face, Hammond turned to a watching official and said 'I reckon this fellow will take 100 wickets this year, and I think he'll play for England one day.'

Prophetic words indeed, as Cook finished the 1946 season with 113 wickets in Championship cricket to earn both his County cap, and after some prompting from Hammond, a place in the second Test Trial at Canterbury in mid-July.

In 1947, Cook was chosen to play for the MCC at Lord's against the touring South Africans, and he celebrated with a second innings return of 6-44, including three in eleven deliveries, as the tourists lost by 158 runs. A fortnight later he took 9-42 against Yorkshire at Bristol, with his victims including Len Hutton, and the England captain Norman Yardley, and it came as no surprise when

Sam won a place in the England side for the First Test with the South Africans at Trent Bridge.

However, it proved to be a frustrating debut as the wicket at Nottingham was very docile, giving little help to any of the bowlers. Sam tried too hard to secure a wicket, lost his customary accuracy, and returned the uncharacteristic figures of 0-127 in 30 overs. His performance confirmed the fears of County colleague Tom Goddard, who had advised Sam to cry off sick rather than making his debut on such a featherbed.

But Sam was an honest cricketer, and felt duty-bound to turn out at Trent Bridge. But perhaps he should have listened to Goddard, as after this modest performance, the selectors called up Doug Wright for the Second Test. The Kent leg-spinner responded with 10 wickets in a comprehensive English victory, and then later in the series, the selectors turned to another spinner, Jack Young of Middlesex. Despite Sam's haul of 138 wickets for Gloucestershire, his performance at Trent Bridge was still in the minds of the selectors and he was overlooked for the winter tour of the Caribbean, Yorkshire's Johnny Wardle being chosen instead.

Sam never played at Test level again, but he continued to be a prolific wicket-taker at County level, taking over a hundred wickets on nine occasions, including 139 wickets in 1950 and 149 at just 14 apiece in 1956. With immaculate length and skilful flight, Cook loved the battle of wits with opposing batsmen, and after deceiving them into playing and missing, he would look up the pitch at them with a quizzical and wicked smile on his face. He was an excellent foil to Tom Goddard, with whom he bowled countless overs in tandem, and his low trajectory and cunning variations of pace and spin made him an extremely difficult bowler for a batsman to score runs off, conceding barely two runs an over throughout his career.

Sam had few pretensions to batting, and for several years had more wickets than runs to his name. His favourite stroke (some might say his only one) was a rather rustic flail – a stroke which Sam dubbed 'the Tetbury chop'. His colleagues, however, were less generous, describing it as the sort of blow a rat catcher would make when trying to kill a rodent!

At the end of the 1964 season, Sam retired and joined the first-class umpire's list. He soon became one of the most respected and popular umpires on the County circuit, showing the same unflappable approach to umpiring that he had shown for so many years of bowling.

By the time he retired in 1986, cricket had become a very different game, and a far cry indeed from his early days where he would leave his home in Tetbury and catch the seven o'clock bus down to Bristol, unsure of how he would return later in the day. For many years, it was commonplace for Colonel Henson, the County's secretary to ask over the loudspeaker 'If anyone is going home Tetbury way, Cook would be very grateful for a lift.' On occasions, however, he was not so fortunate. In his own words, 'if I was still in the field at half past six, I reckoned I'd had it and would have to take the bus to Malmesbury and then walk the five miles back home. But this was not as bad as when we were playing at Cheltenham, as I would have to get off at Kingscote and then walk the seven miles home.' And all that after bowling 30 or 40 overs!

James Cranston
LHB & LM, 1876-1899

Born: 9 January 1859, Bordesley, Birmingham
Died: 10 December 1904, Bristol

Batting

M	I	NO	Runs	Av
103	168	17	3102	20.54
50	100	ct/st		
12	5	46		

Bowling

Balls	Runs	Wkts	Av	5wI	10wM
24	19	0	-	-	-

Best Performances
152 v Yorkshire at Dewsbury, 1890

Had James Cranston not been severely affected by illness, he would surely have won more than just one Test cap, and would probably have established himself as one of Gloucestershire's most prolific amateur batsmen in the early 1900s.

The gifted left-handed batsman from Taunton College made his County debut in 1876, and after finishing school the lithe colt regularly appeared for Gloucestershire. He had a fine match in 1883 against Lancashire, sharing a stand of 126 for the fourth wicket with W.G. Grace. For his part, Cranston made 127 as the County won by six wickets.

Shortly afterwards, he moved to the Midlands, where he played for Worcestershire and Warwickshire, before returning to the West Country in 1889. Despite the fact that he had put on weight, he showed that he not lost his silky touch with the bat, nor his appetite for runs.

Cranston played a host of fine innings in 1889, driving strongly on both sides of the wicket and playing defensively with the straightest of straight bats. He made centuries against Sussex at Hove and Surrey at Cheltenham with his 111* in the latter game being even more impressive given that only one other batsman all summer took a hundred off the crack Surrey bowlers.

In 1889, he was almost as prolific as W.G., and they shared a partnership that gave Gloucestershire a famous victory over Yorkshire at Dewsbury, Cranston hitting a career-best 152.

His efforts with the bat led to him being put forward as the leading left-hander in England,

and with Peel, Ulyett and Stoddart unavailable to play against Australia at The Oval, the Surrey committee (who selected the side for The Oval Tests) invited him to play in the Test. Despite being played on a damp wicket, it proved to be a fine game, with England winning a tense encounter as Cranston played his part, despite only making 16 and 15. In the first innings, he stubbornly defended against the hostile pace of Turner and Ferris before running himself out. Then in the second innings, when England went in to get 95, Cranston and Maurice Read shared a match winning partnership, taking the score from 32-4 to 83-5, and despite another clatter of wickets, England won with two wickets in hand.

It seemed that Cranston was destined for a fine career at Test level, but in June 1891 he suffered an epileptic fit and was carried from the field and received medical treatment from W.G. and E.M. Grace in the changing rooms, before being taken away for further treatment. He was well enough to travel to Taunton the following month to play against Somerset, but after losing form, and feeling groggy, he underwent further treatment.

Sadly, he was unable to play County cricket for eight years, and by the time he was well enough to play club cricket again, he was even more portly, and unable to fully exert himself in the field, in case the sudden exercise prompted another seizure. In 1899, he was well enough to play for four matches, but by now he had lost his touch with the bat. Tragically, within five years he died, his talents largely unfulfilled.

John Frederick Crapp

LHB, 1936-1956

Born: 14 October 1912, St Columb Major, Cornwall
Died: 13 February 1981, Knowle

Batting

M	I	NO	Runs	Av
422	708	73	22195	34.95
50	100	ct/st		
127	36	366		

Bowling

Balls	Runs	Wkts	Av	5wI	10wM
460	306	6	51.00	-	-

Best Performances

175 v Cambridge University at Fenner's, 1947
3-24 v Leicestershire at Leicester, 1937

The chance to represent your country is the highest accolade a sportsman can receive. Like many debutants, Jack Crapp could have been forgiven for having the odd butterfly in the pit of his stomach as he strode to the wicket in the Ashes series of 1948, proudly wearing his first England cap, and becoming the first Cornishman to play Test cricket for England.

But on that particular day at Old Trafford, he could have had an extra reason for being wary as he arrived at the crease after England's master batsman, Denis Compton, had been forced to retire hurt after being hit by a bouncer from Ray Lindwall. It therefore spoke volumes for Jack's composure that he calmly played himself in, and put out of his mind the images of 'Compo' being helped to the dressing rooms, bleeding profusely from a deep gash in his forehead.

He was eventually dismissed for 37, but met with less success in the next two Tests – at Leeds he took two catches at slip, but he also uncharacteristically spilled a chance from Don Bradman at a vital stage in the match. Jack was renowned as one of the safest fielders in the country, but this reputation was worth nothing as the Australian maestro went on to make an unbeaten 173 and steer his side to an astonishing total of 404-3 to win the game. He was not the only man to make a lapse in the field, but even so, Jack was omitted for the Fifth Test

at The Oval. However, at a late hour, Jack was recalled when Cyril Washbrook was injured, only to be dismissed for a duck as well as being hit on the head by a ball from Keith Miller that left the doughty Cornishman with a long-lasting headache.

Despite these failures, he won a place in the tour party to South Africa the following winter, and hit half centuries in the Second, Third and Fourth Tests, as well as leading the run chase in the Fifth Test at Port Elizabeth. Even so, this was Jack's final appearance in England colours, and it spoke volumes for the depth of English batting that the selectors could ignore the claims of the staunch left-hander, who had passed a thousand in fourteen of the previous fifteen seasons. Contemporaries believe that Jack's best years were lost to the war, although they believe that both the presence and persona of Wally Hammond may also have had a stultifying effect on Jack's blossoming career.

The quiet Cornishman was happy to play in Hammond's shadow and, sometimes, Jack was inhibited by his presence and single-mindedness. Jack would have loved a word of advice from the great batsman, or praise after a promising innings. But Hammond was not inclined to public shows of affection, nor quiet words in private, and Jack could count on the fingers of one hand the occasions when Hammond praised him for his efforts with the bat. It may, therefore, have been no coincidence that Jack's eventual rise to the England ranks, and his most productive season – 2,014 runs in 1949 – both came after Hammond had departed from the scene.

The solidly built and long armed left-hander had made his Gloucestershire debut in the opening match of the 1936 season, and he had 1,052 runs to his name by the end of his first summer in County cricket, including 168 against Sussex. He continued to impress in 1937, with some level-headed displays of batting, as well as some classical off-drives and other glimpses of a more attacking streak in run chases, fully refuting the claims of those who felt he was not enterprising enough in his run scoring.

By the Ashes series of 1938, he was being talked about as a potential Test player, but the following summer, just as he was coming into his prime, the outbreak of war ended any thoughts Jack might have held about forcing his way into the England side. When County cricket resumed in 1946, there were several young pretenders: all eager to secure places in England's middle order. However, Jack was not to be denied the chance of representing his country and his call-up in 1948 followed a gallant three-and-a-half-hour century for Gloucestershire against the Australians, shortly before the Third Test of the series.

In 1951, the popular Jack took a well-deserved Benefit, and in the winter of 1953/54 he visited India with the Commonwealth side, only to return home ill after two matches. By this time, he had become the Gloucestershire's club captain, having taken over the leadership in 1953. It was a measure of his popularity, and the high esteem in which he was held by his colleagues, that the softly spoken and undemonstrative man became the first professional to be appointed as Gloucestershire's captain.

Like his batting, Jack showed a quiet and unruffled approach to captaincy, but he did not really enjoy leadership. His second year in charge saw the County suffer their worst summer for two decades. He himself suffered a barren run of form – and all whilst suffering from a bout of eczema on his hands that was so severe that they were often red raw, with blood sometimes oozing out from his gloves whilst batting.

It was with some relief that Jack stood down at the end of 1954 and handed over the captaincy to his good friend George Emmett.

Two years later, Jack retired from the County game, and in 1957 he joined the first-class umpires list. He soon became a highly respected official and stood in four Tests in the mid-1960s. Crapp remained on the first-class list until ill health forced his retirement at the end of 1978 after standing in over 450 matches.

Born: 15 May 1899, Devenport, Auckland
Died: 2 November 1975, Devenport, Auckland

Batting

M	I	NO	Runs	Av
191	309	17	8271	28.32
50	100	ct/st		
39	16	121/5		

Bowling

Balls	Runs	Wkts	Av	5wI	10wM
444	240	7	34.28	-	-

Best Performances
223 v Worcestershire at Worcester, 1930
2-8 v Middlesex at Lord's, 1933

Few people can claim to have struck the first ball they faced in Championship cricket for six, but this was exactly what Charlie Dacre did after moving from his native New Zealand to play for Gloucestershire – the county where his father had been born.

Dacre had first played for Auckland as a fifteen year old, and on his debut he played in borrowed flannels, having arrived without his kit!

After the First World War, Dacre became a regular member of the Auckland side, and developed a reputation as a ferocious hitter. Small in stature, but strong in the chest and shoulders, his approach to batting was simply that a ball was there to be hit, and he did so with a single-minded purpose and complete abandon.

In 1925, Dacre became the first New Zealander to score a century in each innings of a match, achieving the feat with 127* and 107* for Auckland against Victoria. He was an automatic choice on New Zealand's tour to Australia in 1925/26 and then he was appointed vice-captain on their visit to England in 1927.

But just when his star seemed to be in the ascendancy in New Zealand, Dacre opted to throw his lot in with Gloucestershire. It followed a highly successful tour to England in 1927, which included 176 in two and a quarter hours

against Derbyshire and 64 in twenty-five minutes opening the batting against Gloucestershire at the Cheltenham Festival.

His half-century at Cheltenham impressed the County's officials and they were even more delighted when, after the tour, Dacre enquired about joining them for the 1928 season. After another tour to Australia in 1927/28, Dacre decided to qualify for Gloucestershire. After a spell coaching at the Fry's ground, he turned professional in 1930 and won a regular place in the Gloucestershire side. During his first season, Dacre amassed 1,413 runs, including 223 against Worcestershire, and over the next few seasons, he continued in prolific form, scoring 16 centuries, in addition to keeping wicket in emergencies.

Despite a penchant for making rapid centuries, Dacre was apt to throw his wicket away at crucial moments. His brash outlook and flamboyant approach rather irked Wally Hammond – 'I just cannot get on with that bloody Kiwi,' Hammond would say, with more than a hint of envy at Charlie's self confidence. So strong was the feeling between the two that, in 1933 at Worcester, after Dacre struck his second hundred of the match, Hammond – who himself had made a century in the first innings – made sure that he matched the New Zealander's feat in Gloucestershire's second innings.

In 1936, Dacre badly injured his right arm and was forced to retire from County cricket. He returned to New Zealand, where he subsequently worked as a groundsman in Christchurch.

Jack Davey
LHB & LFM, 1966-1978

Born: 4 September 1944, Tavistock, Devon

Batting

M	I	NO	Runs	Av
175	208	90	918	7.77
148	65	39	134	5.15

50	100	ct/st
1	-	32
-	-	17

Bowling

Balls	Runs	Wkts	Av	5wI	10wM
24354	11720	411	28.51	9	-
7037	4456	170	26.21		

Best Performances
53* v Glamorgan at Bristol, 1977
6-95 v Nottinghamshire at Gloucester, 1967
16 v Somerset at Street, 1975
4-11 v Glamorgan at Lydney, 1975

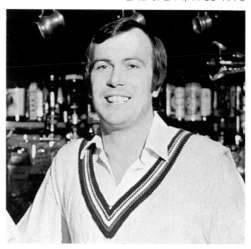

The jovial Jack Davey was a true County professional; the cheerful left-arm bowler from Tavistock claimed over 400 first-class wickets in thirteen seasons of loyal and dependable service to his adopted county.

After two successful seasons for Devon, Davey joined the Gloucestershire staff in 1966 and made his debut later that summer against Cambridge University. In 1967, he recorded a career-best 6-95 against Nottinghamshire at Gloucester, but it was not until 1971, after the retirement of David Smith, that Davey won a regular place in the Championship side and secured his County cap.

Davey developed into a persevering bowler and one with a great heart, often prepared to bowl a long spell, and he had the knack of dismissing the best player in the opposition by getting a ball to nip back in off the pitch. He also became a key member of the County's one-day side, delivering many important spells, including 4-35 against Essex in the quarter-final of the 1973 Gillette Cup. In the semi-final at Worcester, Davey held his nerve when bowling the final over when the home team needed twelve to win. The equation was down to six off the last ball, but Davey calmly fired in a quick straight ball which Ormrod could only pull for a single and Gloucestershire were able to celebrate their first appearance in a Lord's final.

He came up trumps again in the final, taking the vital wicket of Roger Prideaux just as the Sussex batsmen were starting to pick off the Gloucestershire bowlers. Davey's nagging line on middle and leg frustrated Prideaux and, unable to get the ball away, he was bowled attempting a rash stroke. Prideaux's departure boosted Gloucestershire's hopes and although Davey only took one wicket, his accuracy was a key element in his side's 40-run victory.

In 1976, Davey took a hat-trick against Oxford University, but in the following year he only made one Championship appearance and was hampered by an injured Achilles tendon. That combined with ankle problems hastened the end of his County career the following year. Jack had a modest record as a batsman, but the number eleven often claimed, with a broad beam on his face, that his efforts with the bat were not really appreciated. No sooner had he played himself in than he lost his partner at the other end! Joking apart, he played several fine knocks, and in 1973 against Glamorgan at Bristol, added 57 in a quite remarkable final-wicket stand with John Mortimore to win the game.

Indeed, Jack's rustic batting plus his lionhearted and jovial manner made him a firm favourite with Gloucestershire supporters. At Bristol in 1977, Jack delighted his fan club with his only half century in County cricket, as the Glamorgan bowlers toiled again as Davey hit an unbeaten 53*. Each lusty blow stroke was typically played with a broad smile on his face, and in recognition of his efforts, one Gloucestershire member, who was a butcher, presented Jack with a frozen lamb!

Born: 27 April 1879, Upway, Dorset
Died: 15 September 1937, Leckhampton

Batting

M	I	NO	Runs	Av
388	628	244	3966	10.32
50	100	ct/st		
4	-	284		

Bowling

Balls	Runs	Wkts	Av	5wI	10wM
96582	41413	2083	19.88	205	57

Best Performances
71 v Somerset at Taunton, 1909
10-40 v Essex at Bristol, 1906

George Dennett was the first Gloucestershire bowler to take all ten wickets in an innings, with the left-arm spinner returning figures of 19.4-7-40-10 in Essex's first innings of their match at Bristol in August 1906.

On no fewer than twelve occasions, Dennett took over a hundred wickets in a season, and in 1912 he took six wickets for no runs in the space of twenty balls against Kent at Dover. In all, Dennett took over 2,000 wickets with his left-arm spin for Gloucestershire in a highly successful career between 1903 and 1926. But this might not have occurred had the Dorset-born spinner not been spotted by Gilbert Jessop whilst playing in club cricket in Bristol.

Dennett had initially played for the Grange club in Edinburgh, before taking up an appointment in Bristol. In one game, Jessop was amongst the spectators, and after Dennett had made a sublime century and taken a hatful of wickets, Jessop recommended Dennett to the County's selectors. Soon afterwards, he made his debut against Middlesex at Lord's, and he continued to impress Jessop with his steady bowling and unflappable outlook, as Middlesex rattled up 502.

He subsequently became one of the mainstays in the County's attack, and in 1907 at Gloucester, he produced a truly remarkable performance as Northamptonshire were dis-missed for just a paltry 12. Dennett returned the remarkable analysis of 6-1-9-8, including the hat-trick, and had Harry Wrathall not dropped East, he would have taken four in four. When the visitors batted again, Dennett added another seven scalps to finish with 15 wickets for 21 runs – not bad for one day's work !

Dennett was the leading wicket-taker in the country in 1907, taking 201 wickets in all games, including 184 for Gloucestershire in Championship matches, with fourteen wickets against Kent at Cheltenham, and twelve in the games with Yorkshire at Harrogate, Essex at Bristol and Hampshire at Cheltenham.

Dennett had a high, quick arm action, delivering the ball with a bewitching loop, and gaining steep bounce from the surface. This, allied to any turn he extracted, made Dennett one of the most feared bowlers on the County circuit in the years leading up to the First World War. He also had an idiosyncratic way of tilting his head to one side at the moment of release, appearing to watch the ball out of his hand.

During the Boer War, Dennett had served with the Somerset Light Infantry, and whilst in the Cape he had displayed his all-round abilities by playing cricket for the Army at Pretoria, in addition to keeping goal for the services side at Cape Town. He also distinguished himself at fives, billiards and shooting. After retiring from County cricket, Dennett succeeded Billy Woof as coach at Cheltenham College, the scene of many of his fine days in Gloucestershire's colours.

Alfred Ernest Dipper

RHB & RM, 1908-1932

Born: 9 November 1885, Apperley
Died: 7 November 1945, Lambeth, London

Batting

M	I	NO	Runs	Av
478	860	68	27948	35.28

50	100	ct/st		
146	53	210		

Bowling

Balls	Runs	Wkts	Av	5wI	10wM
8882	4903	161	30.45	5	1

Best Performances

252* v Glamorgan at Cheltenham, 1923
7-46 v Leicestershire at Cheltenham, 1919

Alf Dipper had a dramatic entry into County cricket in 1908. The farmer's son had been opening the batting for the Tewkesbury club, characteristically without fuss or flourish, but with great effect, and his name had been touted for County selection.

His call-up duly came as Gloucestershire were due to travel to Tonbridge to play Kent, but they found themselves unable to raise eleven fit players. At the time, 'Dip' was helping on the family's farm near Apperley, and after receiving the summons to travel to Kent, Dipper quickly gathered up his kit into a large brown paper carrier, packed a change of clothes into a small suitcase, and headed off to catch the train. It might have been daunting, but Dipper was not the nervous type, and made an unbeaten 30 on a wicket that was assisting the Kent spinners. His steady batting impressed Charlie Parker, with whom he had played for Tewkesbury, and as he walked off the field, Parker said to him 'Nothing wrong with that, Alf. Looked as though you'd been playing County cricket for years.'

Despite this sound debut, Dipper played just occasionally for the County over the next three seasons. However, in 1911 he was the regular Gloucestershire opener. Dipper subsequently passed a thousand runs and for the next twenty years was the bulwark at the top of the batting order, hitting 53 centuries in all first-class cricket. Between 1912 and 1926, he was the County's leading run scorer in every season bar one.

Dipper had a quite ugly open stance, and he would usually shuffle across his stumps as the ball was bowled, to play the ball off his legs with a series of glances, drives, pulls or hooks. Others may have been more elegant stylists, but 'Old Dip' was the man Gloucestershire could rely on to score vital runs on the most spiteful of pitches. He never worried about his awkward-looking stance, with feet wrongly positioned and his bottom sticking out. As David Foot commented, 'he was an endearing, cussed countryman who got on with his cricket in his own way. The undeniable fact was that in his rural operation of putting bat to ball, devoid of irksome refinement, he seldom played a streaky shot.'

For his part, Dipper was very conscious of the County's modest batting resources in the 1920s, and until the emergence of Wally Hammond, Dipper favoured a cautious rather than an adventurous approach to batting. He therefore rarely gave it away when well set, and during his career, Dipper recorded three double-hundreds, including a majestic 252* against Glamorgan during the 1923 Cheltenham Festival. He also passed 2,000 runs for a season on five occasions, with his most productive season being 1928, when his tally was 2,365 at an average of 55.00.

He was also a purveyor of steady seam bowling, and as befitted a loyal professional, Dipper was always prepared to bowl a few overs to give a

laboured towards the ball, the laconic Parker dryly commented: 'Just look at that – there go my greyhounds!'

While Dipper may not have been the most agile and athletic fielder in Gloucestershire's history, he had a safe pair of gnarled hands, and held over 200 catches for the County. Even so, contemporary writers have hinted that it was his poor fielding that limited Dipper to just a solitary appearance for England in the Ashes series of 1921. His sole Test cap came in the Second Test at Lord's, where he made 11 and 40, but ended up on the losing side as Australia won by 8 wickets. There were some favourable comments about his plucky batting, but the team as a whole were criticised for their poor fielding. One journalist even wrote that 'this must have been one of the worst fielding combinations ever to represent England in a Test match.' Had they not lost the game, and had Dipper been more fleet of foot in the field, the Gloucestershire man might have had a more extended Test career.

Dipper remained a close friend of Charlie Parker, despite the fact that they were extreme opposites in terms of personality. While Dipper was quiet and reserved, Parker was tetchy and outspoken, but cricket was the common bond and their friendship remained loyal and true. In the 1920s, they were the County's two most senior professionals, and when Gloucestershire were faced with difficult away matches, the pair formed an unofficial selection committee. They scoured local papers to see if they could unearth any bowlers who were in form in club cricket, and were worth a gamble on the featherbed wickets elsewhere in the country. Indeed, there are stories that colleagues would often find the pair immersed in the newspapers in the pavilion, with Dipper puffing away on a cigarette, and replying to Parker's suggestions with a broad burr: 'Arr, he'll do. Take 'im up for the next game.'

breather to other bowlers. If Dipper had any weaknesses it was in his fielding, running rather stiffly in the field, and rarely moving in anticipation of a ball being struck to him.

But he was not alone, and on occasion his colleagues seemed to waddle rather than run after the ball. There are a host of humorous stories about the County's fielding, with perhaps the most famous coming from a game in the 1920s when captain Douglas Robinson had an aberration, and placed Dipper and two of the slowest fielders to guard the leg side to Charlie Parker's bowling. When the batsman hit the ball past square leg, all three of the fielders remained motionless, leaving it to each other. But as the ball slowed down approaching the boundary, they each set off in turn towards it. As they

Dipper lost his place in the Gloucestershire side in 1931, and he retired from the County game during the following summer to join the first-class umpires list. This was not an end to his sporting career, as Dipper became a celebrated bowls and billiards player. During the Second World War, he moved to London. He was living in Lambeth when he was taken gravely ill and died, two days before his sixtieth birthday.

George Malcolm Emmett
RHB & RM, 1936-1959

Born: 2 December 1912, Agra, India
Died: 18 December 1976, Knowle, Somerset

Batting

M	I	NO	Runs	Av
454	770	44	22806	31.41

50	100	ct/st
126	34	265

Bowling

Balls	Runs	Wkts	Av	5wl	10wM
3730	2455	57	43.07	2	-

Best Performances
188 v Kent at Bristol, 1950
6-137 v Surrey at Bristol, 1938

Only six batsmen have scored more runs for Gloucestershire in first-class cricket than George Emmett and, given his fine record, it is remarkable that he only won a single cap for England.

The son of a British serviceman in India, Emmett was initially on the MCC groundstaff before playing Minor County cricket for Devon between 1932 and 1935. His sound batting and accurate left-arm spin for Torquay CC initially attracted the attention of Somerset, but in 1936 Emmett joined Gloucestershire, who viewed him as a possible successor to Charlie Parker. He duly made his debut against the Indian tourists at Cheltenham, and after qualifying for the County, Emmett won a regular place in the Gloucestershire side in 1938.

The Second World War halted his development, as Emmett saw active service as a sergeant with the Royal Artillery in the North African campaign and in Sicily. After a modest summer in 1946, Emmett returned to form in 1947 and really came into his own as a fine opening batsman. Over the next decade, he became the mainstay of Gloucestershire's top order, passing a thousand runs on 14 occasions, and in 1949, he amassed 2,005 runs.

Despite his slight frame, Emmett regularly unfurled some powerfully struck shots, and pleased the crowd with some beautiful displays of stroke-play. With a high back-lift and full follow-through, he was a most elegant batsman to watch, and he thrilled the supporters with his aggressive and fluent innings. He was a firm believer in the adage that bowlers do well when you let them, and less well when they are getting a bit of stick, and an example of his positive outlook was a brilliant 141 against the 1953 Australians at Bristol.

Emmett's love of dominating the bowlers had already attracted the attention of the England selectors during the Ashes series of 1948, and for the Third Test at Old Trafford, they called up Emmett to partner Cyril Washbrook.

The new pairing had a nightmare start as they narrowly survived a run-out off the first ball of the match. After this unnerving start, Emmett never got into his stride, and the Gloucestershire man had his mettle fully tested by the Australian pace bowlers. With just ten runs to his name, he lost sight of a short lifting ball from Lindwall, and spooned a catch to short-leg. Emmett then had the misfortune to fall to the first ball he faced from Lindwall in the second innings, with wicketkeeper Don Tallon making a fine diving catch to his right to cling on to a thick edge.

The selectors duly recalled Hutton for the Fourth Test at Headingley, but Emmett was still in the selectors' thoughts. Despite not being in the original twelve, he was subsequently called up as cover and travelled up to Leeds. It proved to be a fruitless trip, as Hutton, on his home soil, compiled two half centuries and shared in a pair of century partnerships with Washbrook to nullify the Australian pace attack. Despite

Emmett's wonderful innings saw Gloucester-shire to 417-8, and a first innings lead of 101. The visiting batsmen were then in complete disarray against the Gloucestershire spinners John Mortimore and Sam Cook as Worcestershire were dismissed for 74 to give Gloucestershire an innings victory.

Emmett also showed his prowess on turning wickets by having two successful tours of India with the Commonwealth XI in 1950/51 and 1953/54. On his first tour of the sub-continent, he scored 1,296 runs in all of the first-class games, and filled the number three berth in all of the five unofficial 'Tests' against India.

Emmett captained Gloucestershire from 1955 until 1958, leading by example and proving to be a firm and shrewd leader. His approach to captaincy was quite imaginative on the field, whilst off the field he was a strong and authori-tative figure, earning the nickname of 'Captain Bligh' from the junior players, who also called the team's kit van 'The Bounty'! However, rather than being austere and remote from the needs of his team, Emmett was eager to promote the development of the younger cricketers. He dropped down into the middle order in the interest of his side, and was always prepared to pass on a word of advice.

Despite feeling the odd twinge of arthritis, Emmett continued to be a steady and reliable batsman, but in 1958 he lost form, and in August announced that he would be retiring at the end of the season. There was however, still enough time for one more match-winning salvo, fittingly in the final game of the season. Emmett struck a memorable 127 at Bristol to lead his team to a three-wicket victory over Lancashire, and he left the County Ground to a standing ovation from both the crowd and the opponents.

He was subsequently appointed as Second XI captain in 1959, but an injury in mid-June to Tom Graveney saw his return to captain the First XI. For a while it looked as though it would be a fairytale tale return, as Gloucestershire made an exciting, but ultimately unsuccessful, bid to become County Champions. After a brief spell as coach, firstly for the County and then at Cheltenham College, Emmett became general secretary at the Imperial Athletic Club in Bristol, and he subsequently oversaw their affairs with characteristic efficiency and panache.

Emmett's fine County record and his prolific run scoring, he was never called up again.

There were few better batsmen of spin bowling in the 1950s than Emmett, and perhaps his finest ever innings was 146 against Worcestershire on a turning wicket at Cheltenham in 1951. Despite the spiteful wicket, Emmett completely mastered the spin attack of Roly Jenkins and Dick Howorth, time and again sweeping the Worcestershire spinners off their length. In one over, he hit Jenkins for three successive bound-aries, much to the delight of the large Festival crowd. As the applause died down, Jenkins turned to the Gloucestershire maestro and said 'Emmett, if you don't like me, that's fair enough. But for God's sake, don't keep taking it out on the ball!'

Born: 21 November 1952, Salford Priors

Batting

M	I	NO	Runs	Av
91	150	15	2512	18.60
128	*100*	*12*	*1333*	*15.15*

50	100	ct/st		
6	5	39		
-	3	34		

Bowling

Balls	Runs	Wkts	Av	5wI	10wM
54	40	0	-	-	-

Best Performances

126 v Hampshire at Gloucester, 1979
73 v Somerset at Street, 1975*

In the opinion of many supporters, Jim Foat was one of the finest cover fielders ever to appear for Gloucestershire. The bespectacled former pupil of Millfield School played for the County between 1972 and 1979, and his quick-silver reactions added a valuable new dimension to the County's fielding in one-day games. This helped to overcome some of the limitations of older, more experienced players who were less agile in the field.

His finest moment in an all-too-brief County career was the crucial run out of Tony Greig at a most important phase of the 1973 Gillette Cup final. Greig had arrived at the wicket with his side on 155-3, and needing 94 in the remaining 16 overs. But as Greig tried to steal a leg bye in the first over of Mike Procter's comeback spell, the agile Foat swooped in from cover to run out the Sussex captain before he could get back into his crease. None of the other Sussex batsmen could cope with the bowling of Knight and Procter, and Gloucestershire were able to celebrate their first major success since 1877.

Earlier in match, Foat had also shared in an invaluable partnership of 49 with Tony Brown that helped to lift Gloucestershire spirits after the side slumped to 180-6. Foat ran like a hare between the wickets as Brown launched a furious assault on the Sussex bowlers to see Gloucestershire to a more respectable total of 248-8. His magnificent seven earned Foat a standing ovation from the Lord's crowd and, given the eventual outcome of the match, it was one of the most important sevens in the club's history!

Foat played another little cameo with the bat four years later as Gloucestershire beat Kent to win the 1977 Benson & Hedges Cup but, overall, his batting never really took off. He had quite a productive summer in 1978, with centuries in successive innings against Glamorgan and Warwickshire. The following June, he struck 126 against Hampshire at Gloucester to win his County cap. After this career-best score, it seemed as if Foat had turned the corner, but sadly his form and confidence completely fell away and he left the County's staff at end of season.

Thomas William John Goddard

RHB & RFM/OB, 1922-1952

Born: 1 October 1900, Gloucester
Died: 22 May 1966, Gloucester

Batting

M	I	NO	Runs	Av
558	743	207	5026	9.37
50	100	ct/st		
4	-	300		

Bowling

Balls	Runs	Wkts	Av	5wI	10wM
135115	56061	2862	19.58	245	85

Best Performances
71 v Essex at Southend, 1932
10-113 v Worcestershire at Cheltenham, 1937

Like many great off-spinners, Tom Goddard started life in County cricket as a tearaway fast bowler. The tall youngster from Gloucester made his County debut in 1922 and two years later claimed a hat-trick against Sussex at Eastbourne. However, he lost his way over the next few seasons, proving wayward and expensive, and in 1927 it seemed his County career was over.

But Bev Lyon, his Gloucestershire colleague, believed that Goddard's tall frame, big hands and long, powerful fingers could help him develop into an off-spinner. Goddard subsequently secured a place on the MCC groundstaff in 1928. After being highly impressed by Goddard in the nets at Lord's, Lyon recommended his return to the Gloucestershire staff for 1929.

It proved to be an almost miraculous conversion as Goddard took 175 wickets for Gloucestershire in his first season as a spin bowler and formed a highly effective partnership with the left-arm spin of Charlie Parker. Their finest hour as a spin combination came in the thrilling match with the Australian tourists at Bristol in 1930, shortly after the tourists had won the Ashes at The Oval. Chasing 118 to win, they were pegged down by the accuracy and guile of the Gloucestershire spinners. Wickets fell at regular intervals and, amongst rising excitement, Goddard trapped Hornibrooke leg before as the Australians ended one run short and the game ended in a dramatic tie, with Goddard finishing with match figures of 10-126.

By this time, Goddard had already risen to the ranks of Test cricket. Making his debut in the Fourth Test of the 1930 Ashes series at Old Trafford and getting another mammoth haul of 141 wickets, he won a place on the tour to South Africa in the winter of 1930/31. In fact, after his conversion to spin in 1929, Goddard never failed to take 100 wickets in a season until 1951, when he was struck down with pneumonia and pleurisy. On four occasions he captured over 200 first-class wickets, with 1937 being his most prolific season as he bagged 248 victims in all cricket, and had a quite remarkable strike rate of a wicket every six overs.

A man of few words, he let the ball do the talking for him. He revelled in tricking and teasing the batsman, or bowling around the wicket in search for the inside edge into the hands of one of the three short-legs he regularly employed. But if the batsman was hit on the pads in front of the wicket, Goddard would quickly turn around to roar in his booming baritone voice 'How were 'ee?' As one of his colleagues fondly remembered, 'for Tom, an appeal was always more of a personal demand – one which an umpire new to the list could not refuse, and what is more, Tom did not expect any umpire to refuse. To Tom, they all looked plumb in front!'

Goddard was a huge spinner of the ball, once bowling Patsy Hendren with a ball that pitched at least a foot outside the off-stump and then spun alarmingly to hit the leg stump. With his huge fingers wrapped around the ball, he was capable of making the ball fizz dramatically, as well as lift alarmingly up from the surface. His metronomic command of length and subtle changes of flight meant that even on the easiest of surfaces, batsmen found it difficult to play him with any ease. For his part, Goddard always had an attacking outlook, never considering maiden overs to be of any importance. Bowling defensively was never an option in his mind, and when playing for England, he found it quite difficult at times to follow his captain's instructions of keeping the runs down.

One example of this occurred in the Second Test of the 1937 series against New Zealand at Old Trafford. The Kiwis had made a good start in their pursuit of 265 to win, so when Walter Robins tossed the ball to Goddard, he simply said to the spinner 'Just keep them quiet, Tom.' Goddard was rather taken aback by this. After a modest over, he spoke to his County colleague, Charles Barnett, as the English fielders changed positions before the next over. 'What's up Tom?' said Barnett, to which a rather bemused Goddard replied 'He wants me to keep them quiet and I can't get them out if I don't pitch it up.'

Aware that Goddard, in his first Test for seven years, wanted to create a good impression, Barnett soothed his mind, saying 'Don't worry about that, Tom. They'll be all the quieter once they are back in the pavilion. Just try to bowl them out as if it were a County match.'

His words did the trick as in the space of the next 13 overs, Goddard took 6-29 and England won the match by 130 runs. These were Goddard's best-ever figures for England, and the match-winning spell ensured that he kept his place for the third and final Test of the summer.

Despite a haul of 248 wickets in 1937, Goddard could not force his way back into the England side the following year for the Ashes series. He was included in the thirteen for the Third Test at Old Trafford, but heavy rain led to the match being washed out. He finished the summer with 109 wickets to his name and was nominated as one of *Wisden*'s Five Cricketers of the Year. He won a place on the England winter tour to South Africa, where he won a further three Test caps, and in the First Test of the series over the Christmas period at Johannesburg, Goddard celebrated Boxing Day by claiming a hat-trick in South Africa's first innings.

This was one of five occasions when Goddard recorded a hat-trick with his off-spin. Amongst his other notable returns were 17 wickets in a day against Kent at Bristol in 1939. His career-best performance came in 1937, when he took 10-113 against Worcestershire at Cheltenham in 1937. He benefited from the new lbw law, and ended the season with a County record of 222 wickets to his name – a feat he subsequently repeated ten years later in 1947, aged forty-nine. During a quite remarkable summer, he twice took a hat-trick, against Glamorgan at Swansea and Somerset at Bristol, to finish top of the national bowling average. He repeated the latter in 1949, and during the summer took 15-107 to guide the County to an innings victory over Derbyshire.

He announced his retirement at the end of the 1951 season, after struggling with illness, and established a successful furniture company in Gloucester. But when Mortimore and Wells were away on National Service in 1952, he came back into the County game and claimed 45 wickets in 13 matches. By the time he hung up his boots at the end of the 1952 season, Goddard had no less than 2,979 wickets. He was eager to take another 21 wickets to reach the coveted 3,000 mark, but ill health and the emergence of younger, fitter bowlers prevented this.

Edward Mills Grace

RHB & RFM (and slow under-arm), 1870-1896

Born: 28 November 1841, Downend, Bristol
Died: 20 May 1911, Park House, Thornbury

Batting

M	I	NO	Runs	Av
253	445	11	7859	18.10
50	100	ct/st		
35	3	271		

Bowling

Balls	Runs	Wkts	Av	5wI	10wM
8273	4020	171	23.50	4	-

Best Performances
122 v Lancashire at Clifton, 1882
7-46 v Surrey at Clifton, 1875

Before W.G. Grace first shot to fame as a cricketer, his elder brother, Edward Mills, was widely acknowledged to be the finest all-round cricketer in the country. As it turned out, E.M.'s success spurred W.G. on to bigger and better things, and from 1871 their success with bat and ball made Gloucestershire a first-class club both in name and deeds.

E.M. was encouraged by his parents to play from a young age in the orchard adjoining their home, and from his early teens he played alongside his father and family friends for the West Gloucestershire side. The young lad frequently excelled in the field, and against the All England Eleven, the thirteen year old was presented with a bat by William Clarke after a wonderful performance as long stop.

In 1862, he came to national prominence when, as a late replacement in the MCC side against the Gentlemen of Kent at the Canterbury, he thrilled the Festival side with an unbeaten 192 and then claimed all ten wickets in the home team's second innings.

Like his famous brother, he entered the medical profession and during the late 1860s he cut back on his cricket commitments as he trained to be a surgeon. However, 'The Coroner' returned to major matches in the 1870s following the formation of the County club, for whom he diligently acted as the club's secretary until 1909. He joined his brothers W.G. and

G.F. in the Gloucestershire side and played many more entertaining innings, including 108 against Surrey at The Oval in 1872, enjoying playing cross-batted shots to straight balls to the frustration of the bowler. Indeed, E.M. was one of the first batsmen to specialise in the pull shot, often played with a cocked left leg.

In 1880, despite the fact that his best years were behind him, he was still good enough to be chosen to play for England against Australia at The Oval, and in opening the batting with W.G., the pair added 91 for the first wicket. In 1882, he also hit two further centuries for Gloucestershire with 108 against Somerset and 122 in the match with Lancashire.

E.M. had a cheery outlook on life, full of enthusiasm for the game, and was once described as 'overflowing with cricket at every pore, full of lusty life, cheerily gay with energy inexhaustible.' But like W.G. he also had a quick temper, and whilst batting at Bristol in 1896 with an infected thumb, his pedestrian progress attracted several ribald comments from the crowd. These infuriated E.M., who was in great pain, and he became so enraged by a barracker that he dropped his bat, grabbed a stump and chased the man out of the ground and down the road.

E.M. retired from County cricket in 1896, but continued to play club cricket for Thornbury into the 1900s. In 1909, his lobs brought him 119 wickets. However, the following year, his last in cricket, he had to be carried unconscious from the field, after collapsing from exhaustion.

George Frederick Grace
RHB & RFM, 1870-1880

Born: 13 December 1850, Downend, Bristol
Died: 22 September 1880, Basingstoke

Batting

M	I	NO	Runs	Av
85	129	13	3279	28.26
50	100	ct/st		
15	4	85		

Bowling

Balls	Runs	Wkts	Av	5wI	10wM
9217	3215	167	19.25	8	3

Best Performances
180* v Surrey at Clifton, 1875
8-43 v Yorkshire at Sheffield, 1876

Fred Grace was the fifth and youngest of the Grace brothers, and the tall and muscular member of Gloucestershire's most famous cricketing family seemed destined to follow in his illustrious brothers' footsteps. In 1880, he played alongside E.M. and W.G. in the First Test against Australia at The Oval. Even though he bagged a pair, many believed that Fred would have a fine career, but shortly after that Test, he caught pneumonia and died a few days later.

Fred Grace was considered by contemporaries to have been a more attractive batsman than his older brothers. However, the youngster lacked the concentration and tremendous resolve that allowed E.M. and above all W.G. to build huge innings. Many hoped that as he matured, young Fred might learn these habits that his brothers had put to such good use, but despite many cameo innings for Gloucestershire, he only hit four centuries, with the highlight being 180* against Surrey at Clifton in 1875.

He was also an effective round-arm fast bowler, and his all-round skills were invaluable on the 1873/74 tour to Australia, when a party of English cricketers, plus W.G.'s newly-wedded wife, undertook a long and quite tiring tour 'down under'. It proved to be a fruitful one for Fred, who hit a sparkling 154 against a XXII of Southern Tasmania. While in Tasmania, he made many friends and even missed some later matches in order to visit his new acquaintances. So smitten was Fred by Tasmania, and its ladies, that he vowed that he would settle there one day.

But the tour was not all love and roses, as Fred was hit on the head while playing on a bad wicket at Castlemaine, as well as being on the receiving end in several games of some poor umpiring decisions and ribald comments from the Australian press. He also suffered a bout of quincy and it spoke volumes for Fred's fitness and approach to the game that after this illness, as well as so much travel and junketing, he was prepared to bowl long spells in the intense heat.

Fred was also an excellent fielder in the deep, taking many outstanding catches, as in the 1880 Test with Australia when he memorably held onto a soaring hit from George Bonnor. Legend has it that the batsmen had turned for their third run when the steepler landed in Fred's hands, after he had run towards the edge of the playing area to get right underneath the towering hit.

What made his efforts more remarkable was that Fred had a heavy cold. A few days later, he played for United South at Stroud and was soaked by heavy showers. He briefly spent time at Downend recuperating before playing in a Benefit match at Winchester. It would have been prudent to pull out, but that was not the Grace way, and he travelled to Basingstoke, where his health quickly deteriorated. News of his death shocked the cricket world. Over 3,000 people attended his funeral and fine tributes were paid to Fred.

William Gilbert Grace

RHB & RM, 1870-1899

Born: 18 July 1848, Downend, Bristol
Died: 23 October 1915, Mottingham, Kent

Batting

M	I	NO	Runs	Av
360	612	49	22808	40.51
50	**100**	ct/st		
109	50	376/4		

Bowling

Balls	Runs	Wkts	Av	5wI	10wM
62134	24745	1338	18.49	112	29

Best Performances

318* v Yorkshire at Cheltenham, 1876
9-55 v Nottinghamshire at Cheltenham, 1877

Dr W.G. Grace was the greatest name in Gloucestershire cricket in the nineteenth century and more than a hundred years after his final Test appearance, he still remains one of the most famous, and instantly-recognised, figures in English cricket. His wonderful batting and skilful bowling drew crowds from far and wide, and he became the best known public figure in England apart from Queen Victoria and Mr Gladstone. Indeed, 'The Doctor' did much to popularise cricket as a mass spectator sport – and at a time when the improved railway lines, and rising incomes, gave more and more people the chance to go and watch their heroes in the flesh.

His emergence came at a pivotal time in the game's development as several northern organisations had threatened the dominance of Lord's. As Simon Rae wrote about W.G., 'he was the man the crowds wanted to see. In throwing in his lot with the M.C.C., he effectively headed off a schism and handed the control of the game back to the Lord's establishment.'

If not the inventor of modern batting techniques, he was their greatest early exponent, taking the art of batting to a new level. His record-breaking feats included becoming the first player to score a triple hundred in Championship cricket, with 318* against Yorkshire at Cheltenham, and being the first to amass over two thousand runs in a season, with 2739 runs in 1871. He was also the first player to make a hundred hundreds in first-class cricket.

W.G. was also an outstanding bowler – initially as a round-arm quickie, and later as a cunning bowler of slow-medium pace, relying on flight and guile rather than pace. In 1874, he became the first player to perform the 'Double' and on sixteen occasions he took 8 or more wickets in an innings. In 1877, he had record match figures of 17-89 against Nottinghamshire, and there were fourteen occasions when he scored a century and took ten or more wickets in the game.

Such efforts for both Gloucestershire and England resulted in Grace being called 'The Champion'. With his striking appearance and formidable personality, W.G. became the game's first superstar, and the country's first sportsman to be known solely by his initials. Even today, objects with images of Grace are keenly sought after by collectors of cricket memorabilia.

Grace was also a brilliant fielder, who in 1868 threw a ball at The Oval for 118 yards, and a fine racquets and tennis player and a founder member of the English Bowls Association. He was also a top-class athlete. On top of this, he had a successful doctor's practice in Thornbury, yet still found time to devote to Gloucestershire cricket.

He had been encouraged by his mother to play cricket at an early age, and shortly after his ninth birthday played for West Gloucestershire against Bedminster. With further encouragement from his elder cricketing brothers, he matured into a competent cricketer at an early age. At the age of fifteen, he faced the best

professional bowlers in England when the All England side played a local XXII on Durdham Down, and compiled a composed 32. The following year, he guested for the South Wales Cricket Club and made 170 against the Gentlemen of Sussex at Hove.

In 1866, he struck his maiden first-class hundred. He went on to score a further 125 hundreds – a staggeringly high number at the time, given the variable nature of many wickets, and a figure over twice as high as recorded by his nearest contemporary. His first major innings in the world of professional cricket came in 1866, when the eighteen year old recorded a double century against Surrey. Two years later, he played what he regarded as his finest innings – an all-run 134 on a very poor wicket at Lord's, whilst playing for the Gentlemen against the Players.

His most productive period was the 1870s. In 1871, he enjoyed a wonderful season, with a record 2,739 runs in first-class cricket, including ten hundreds. In 1873, he scored 1,000 runs and took 100 wickets in the space of eleven games between 6 July and 12 September. In 1875, the Doctor took 191 wickets at 12.92 apiece, having converted to more gentle, crafty slows.

He continued in prolific form in 1876, making an unbeaten 400 in an exhibition match against a XXII of Grimsby. He became Gloucestershire's first batsman to record a triple hundred, with 318* against Yorkshire at Cheltenham. His record-breaking score came during a purple patch in August, which included 344 for MCC against Kent at Canterbury, and 177 against Nottinghamshire at Clifton.

In 1880, he appeared in the first ever Ashes Test in this country, and he hit the Australian attack all around The Oval in making a commanding 152. Even when into his forties, W.G. retained both his appetite for runs and his sharp reflexes, and in 1895, at the age of forty-seven, he hit 1,016 runs in May, including 288 against Somerset and 257 against Kent.

Stories of his gamesmanship are legendary, including the match at Grimsby in 1876 where he batted for three days against a local side, made 399 and persuaded the scorers to add one more run onto his score. Although he was an amateur, W.G. certainly made more money out of the game than the professionals, and used his power to get what he wanted – sometimes only agreeing to play if his financial terms were met. Few people quarrelled with W.G., especially as he had an explosive temper. On occasions, though, his behaviour off the field was far below that expected from a 'gentleman'. However, there was also a kinder side to his character, including the merry way he nurtured young talent.

In 1899, a very public spat took place between Grace and the Gloucestershire committee. The previous summer, he had helped the founders of London County establish first-class games at Crystal Palace and had agreed to act as secretary and manager. He had also resigned from his doctor's practice in Bristol, so, fearing they would lose his services, the committee tactlessly wrote to Grace asking for details of which matches he would be available for. Grace was furious, as he had played in all of their games so far. He sent his resignation, and ended his association with the County.

He continued to play for London County and other first-class sides until 1908. His final innings was an unbeaten 69 for Eltham against Grove Park, just before the First World War.

David Anthony Graveney

RHB & SLA, 1972-1990

Born: 2 January 1953, Westbury-on-Trym, Bristol

Batting

M	I	NO	Runs	Av
379	486	141	6107	17.70
315	*197*	*72*	*1983*	*15.86*
50	100	ct/st		
15	2	202		
1	*-*	*85*		

Bowling

Balls	Runs	Wkts	Av	5wI	10wM
56115	23688	815	29.06	35	6
10543	*7228*	*229*	*31.56*		

Best Performances

119 v Oxford University at Oxford, 1980
8-85 v Nottinghamshire at Cheltenham, 1974
56 v Nottinghamshire at Bristol, 1985*
5-11 v Ireland at Dublin, 1981

David Graveney followed his father, Ken, and uncle, Tom, into the Gloucestershire side in 1972. He subsequently continued the good name of the family, playing with distinction as a left-arm spin bowler, leading the County for eight seasons and becoming one of the current game's leading administrators.

In only his second season of County cricket, Graveney helped Gloucestershire reach the final of the Gillette Cup, impressing with bat and ball, as well as excelling in the field. In the final against Sussex, he took a good catch to dismiss the dangerous Mike Buss.

In 1977, David Graveney added a Benson & Hedges winner's medal to his trophy cabinet when his side beat Kent in the Final at Lord's. However, they might not have reached Lord's had it not been for a fine spell of spin bowling from Graveney, in the quarter-final with Middlesex. In the final, he bowled another steady spell, conceding just 26 runs from his nine overs, in addition to claiming two wickets, including that of Kent's top-scorer Bob Woolmer.

Throughout his career, he proved to be a steady and thoughtful left-arm spinner, cleverly using his height and varying his flight to deceive opponents. He was also capable of keeping things tight in a more defensive mode, as well as on helpful surfaces bowling the classic left armer's delivery of pitching on leg and hitting the top of the off stump. The wickets at Bristol often gave Graveney little help, especially when Courtney Walsh was in his pomp, and slightly more grass was left on the wickets in order to favour the quicker bowlers. Even so, it was at Bristol in 1988 that Graveney produced his best match analysis, 14-165 against Worcestershire.

In 1990 he left to join Somerset, before moving to the north-east to lead Durham in their inaugural season in the County Championship in 1992. During the winter months, he qualified as an accountant, and Graveney has subsequently used these administrative skills in his role as manager of the Mike Gatting 'rebel' tours to South Africa, and later with the Professional Cricketers' Association, and as chairman of the England Selection Panel.

John Kenneth Richard Graveney
LHB & RFM, 1947-1964

Born: 16 December 1924, Hexham

Batting

M	I	NO	Runs	Av
110	165	26	1995	14.35
2	2	0	39	19.50

50	100	ct/st		
5	-	51		
-	-	2		

Bowling

Balls	Runs	Wkts	Av	5wI	10wM
10521	4706	170	27.68	6	1
60	42	-	-		

Best Performances
62 v Leicestershire at Leicester, 1949
10-66 v Derbyshire at Chesterfield, 1949
31 v Surrey at The Oval, 1964

Ken Graveney was the younger brother of Tom, and after leaving Bristol Grammar School, the talented young sportsman became an officer in the Royal Marine Commandos, landing in Normandy at dawn on D-Day in June 1944. After being demobilised, he joined the Gloucestershire staff, ostensibly as a left-handed batsman, and in 1947 he made his County debut against Worcestershire at Gloucester.

However, it was his skill as a fast-medium out-swing bowler that brought Graveney early success at County level, and in 1949 he took all ten Derbyshire wickets for 66 runs in the match at Chesterfield. He was only the fourth Gloucestershire bowler to achieve the feat of taking all ten, and his figures, the second-best in the club's long history, were even more remarkable given the fact that the Queens Park wicket was expected to turn.

In fact, he nearly didn't get chance to bowl, as when Derbyshire began their second innings, 352 runs behind, the plan had been for Gloucestershire to open with their spin bowlers. However, Basil Allen decided to let the seamers have a couple of overs each. With the penultimate ball of his second over, Graveney took his first wicket, so Allen decided to give him another over in the hope that he might get yet another. He duly took a wicket in his third, fourth and fifth over to finish the day's play with 4 for 5.

The following morning, he added another scalp in the first over of the morning, before adding four more as the Derbyshire resistance crumbled. Their final pair, Bill Copson and Les Jackson, then offered stout resistance. As they dug in, Allen told the tiring Graveney he would have only three more overs in which to take his tenth wicket. But Graveney still earned a place in Gloucestershire's record books, as Copson holed out at extra cover to give him his prize.

Sadly, in 1950, Ken started to suffer from spinal disc problems, and he was forced into retirement from the county game. However, he continued to play in club cricket, and by the early 1960s, turned out regularly for the county Second XI, who he captained successfully.

In 1963, Graveney made a dramatic return to the county game, as he replaced Tom Pugh as the club captain. Despite not having played since 1951, he proved to be a capable leader. His team slipped to eighth place, but this was quite a creditable position given a loss of form by other players, a series of injuries and interruptions from the weather. Graveney led the side again in 1964, before handing over to John Mortimore and returning to the business world.

Graveney remained involved with the County, serving initially on the committee, where his business skills were invaluable in the mid-1970s as he helped to extricate the cash-strapped County from a severe financial crisis. Graveney's powers of tact and diplomacy were also recognised with his appointment first as chairman and then as the club's president.

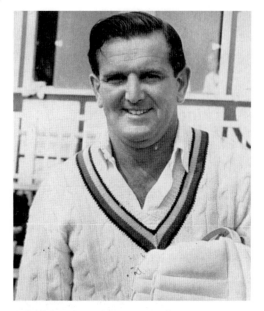

Born: 16 June 1927, Riding Mill, Northumberland

Batting

M	I	NO	Runs	Av
296	506	48	19705	43.02
50	**100**	**ct/st**		
97	50	227		

Bowling

Balls	Runs	Wkts	Av	5wI	10wM
3854	2001	57	35.10	1	-

Best Performances

222 v Derbyshire at Chesterfield, 1954
5-28 v Derbyshire at Bristol, 1953

The batting of Tom Graveney was elegance personified. Between 1948 and 1960, his graceful and cultured batting decorated many Gloucestershire innings, with Tom taking great delight in getting onto the front foot and, with a high flowing backlift, unleashing a host of majestic strokes. His classical and languid off-drives frequently evoked memories of strokes played by Wally Hammond.

Tom was the first post-war batsman in England to score 30,000 runs, and in 1964 he reached the landmark of a hundred hundreds. However, by this time Tom was a Worcester-shire batsman, as his glittering career with Gloucestershire had come to a most unfortunate end in 1960.

Born in Northumberland but educated at Bristol Grammar School, Graveney excelled at both golf and cricket from an early age. As his National Service with the Royal Gloucestershire Regiment drew to a close, he had the opportunity to become an accountant, or a professional golfer. Instead, he opted to follow his elder brother Ken into County cricket, and accepted an offer to join his adopted County in 1948.

The offer followed some promising innings by Second Lieutenant Graveney in charity and benefit matches in 1947, and when Ken Graveney introduced Tom to the other professionals, he said 'this is my kid brother, who I

can't bowl out.' County bowlers were soon of the same opinion, and in every summer from 1949, Tom passed a thousand runs and delighted the home supporters with his classical stroke-play. With the Bristol crowds increasingly talking about the 'new Hammond', Tom's name entered the notebooks of the England selectors.

In 1950, Tom scored 1,772 runs and registered his first double century – 201 against Sussex at Worthing. The following summer, he amassed 2,291 runs with centuries in both innings of match against Northants at Bristol, and he duly made his England debut in the Third Test of the 1951 series against the South Africans at Old Trafford. On the winter tour to India, Tom recorded his maiden Test century, with 175 in the Second Test at Bombay, and he returned from the sub-continent to notch up a further 1515 runs for the County in 1952, and became one of *Wisden*'s Cricketers of the Year.

For the next six years, Graveney was a prolific scorer for Gloucestershire. In 1954, he made 222 against Derbyshire at Chesterfield – his highest score for the County – and two years later he scored 2,397 runs in a truly golden summer. Yet during this period, Graveney was in and out of the England side, with a few people in lofty positions believing that he only scored runs when the going was easy.

Had they seen Graveney bat at Romford in 1954, they would never have had these thoughts. On a spiteful green-top, the Essex bowlers made the ball swing and seam about in a most bewildering fashion as Gloucestershire were dismissed for 153. This held no terrors however for Tom, and the master craftsman compiled a graceful century, undeterred by the vicious movement off the pitch and the lavish swing. In the second innings, he made 67 out of 107, and only two other Gloucestershire batsmen reached double figures in the match.

Amongst his fine performances for England was 231 against British Guiana at Georgetown on the 1953/54 tour to the West Indies, during which Tom and Willie Watson added 402 for the fourth wicket. The following winter, he temporarily lost his place in the Test side on the tour to Australia, critics suggesting that he lost concentration at vital times, and that his front foot technique was not suited to the faster wickets 'down under'. Tom, however, played in the Fifth Test at Sydney and proved the critics wrong with an innings of 111.

However, his most memorable innings in England colours came at Trent Bridge against the 1957 West Indians, where Tom made a majestic 258 at Trent Bridge. Throughout his eight-hour innings, Tom drove with tremendous power, and completely mastered the wiles of the spinners Ramadhin and Valentine during wonderful partnerships with Peter Richardson and Peter May which each amassed over 200 runs.

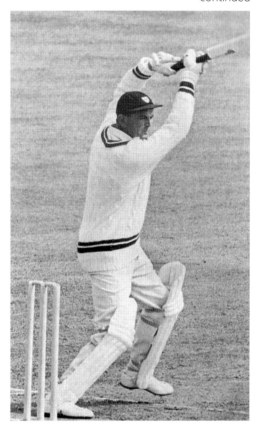

Tom took over the Gloucestershire captaincy in 1959. His team enjoyed a successful year as they finished as runners-up in the Championship, but Tom was troubled by a shoulder injury and he missed ten games. He returned to full fitness in 1960 and shared in the County's record second-wicket stand of 256 against Derbyshire at Chesterfield with Tom Pugh, the Old Etonian amateur. But there was little success on the field, whilst off it, the club failed to improve their financial situation. As Graveney later wrote, 'captaincy is one of those odd, intangible things which you do not choose and which is invariably thrust upon you at the wrong time. In my first spell of it with Gloucestershire, I was an apprentice who had to find out about it in the middle. It could be a trying business. As a young captain I hardly ever decided to do anything without worrying about the consequences if it went wrong.'

At the end of 1960, Tom stood down as captain, and left the club after a very public and unfortunate spat with the County officials, some

of whom seemed eager to blame him for the club's financial situation. These internal wranglings certainly left their mark on a fairly uncomplicated, easy going individual, and many people felt that Tom emerged a more ruthless and less frivolous batsman. After qualifying for Worcestershire, he had a series of vintage seasons for his new County, and in 1964 they won the Championship title.

In 1966, Tom enjoyed a wonderful return to the England Test team, and in 1968 he took over the captaincy of his new County, led England against Australia at Headingley, and was awarded the OBE for his services to cricket. He retired at the end of the 1970 season, before taking up a coaching appointment in Brisbane, where he continued playing first-class cricket until 1971/72. He subsequently returned to the UK and became landlord of The Royal Oak pub near Cheltenham racecourse. Tom has also become a respected summariser on television and radio, and is still active in supporting cricketing causes.

David Michael Green

RHB & RM, 1968-1973

Born: 10 November 1939, Llanengan

Batting

M	I	NO	Runs	Av
81	146	1	4703	32.43
54	54	1	1308	24.68

50	100	ct/st
25	7	36
6	1	10

Bowling

Balls	Runs	Wkts	Av	5wl	10wM
984	475	9	52.77	-	-
1544	960	45	21.33		

Best Performances

233 v Sussex at Hove, 1968
4-61 v Surrey at The Oval, 1968
127* v Hampshire at Bristol, 1970
4-21 v Surrey at The Oval, 1969

David Green had an illustrious record with Lancashire and Oxford University, and in 1965 he achieved the feat of scoring 2,000 runs during the season without hitting a hundred. In 1968, he joined Gloucestershire, where his bold hitting enlivened many innings, and with the Sunday League starting in 1969, he proved to be a valuable acquisition to the County's ranks. In 1970, he hit the County's first century at home in the competition with a typically rousing 127* off 104 balls against Hampshire at Bristol.

Green had an immediate impact following his move to the West Country, and in 1968 he scored over 2,000 runs to win his County cap and become one of *Wisden*'s Five Cricketers of the Year. Such riches looked distant at the start of the season, as his first sixteen innings yielded a mere 224 runs. But after some useful advice from George Emmett and Arthur Milton, there was a metamorphosis. Green moved up to open the batting, and he and Milton established a new club record opening partnership at Hove with 315 against Sussex, Green finishing on 233 after nearly six hours at the crease.

Green finished 1968 as the County's leading run scorer in Championship cricket, and in 1969 he passed a thousand once again, in addition to making some forthright contributions with the bat, plus some nagging spells of medium pace in limited-overs games. Once again, it was Sussex who were on the receiving end of Green's talents, this time with ball in hand, as he returned a spell of 8-4-8-2 at Lydney.

Born in Caernarvonshire, Green spent his early life in Cheshire, before becoming a schoolboy prodigy at Manchester Grammar School, playing cricket for Lancashire Second Eleven, as well as rugby for Sale and later Cheshire. He went up to Oxford to read history, winning blues in 1959, 1960 and 1961, and playing for Lancashire in his university vacations.

Green joined the Lancashire staff on a full-time basis in 1962, immediately won his cap, and then in 1965 made his record-breaking aggregate of 2,000. After being released by Lancashire at the end of 1967, he agreed to play cricket for Gloucestershire, as well as rugby for Bristol. The move to the West Country revitalised his career and thirst for runs, with his aggressive and lusty batting, evoking memories amongst older members of Charles Barnett and other greats of a bygone era.

He retired from first-class cricket in 1971, and later moved into journalism, covering cricket and rugby for *The Daily Telegraph*. This has proved to be an ideal medium for Green, with his keen intellect and encyclopaedic memory for statistics and achievements. A witty conversationalist, he has become an astute summariser for BBC Radio Wales cricket programmes.

Walter Reginald Hammond
RHB & RFM/RM, 1920-1951

Born: 19 June 1903, Buckland, Dover, Kent
Died: 1 July 1965, Kloof, Natal, South Africa

Batting

M	I	NO	Runs	Av
405	664	74	33664	57.05
50	100	ct/st		
122	113	552		

Bowling

Balls	Runs	Wkts	Av	5wI	10wM
33746	14801	504	29.36	15	3

Best Performances
317 v Nottinghamshire at Gloucester, 1936
9-23 v Worcestershire at Cheltenham, 1928

Wally Hammond was probably the greatest figure in Gloucestershire cricket after W.G. Grace. Indeed, when contemporaries have been asked the question 'Who was the finest cricketer that you ever saw or played against?' the answer has invariably been Wally Hammond. With over 50,000 runs to his name, including 167 centuries, only five other batsmen have scored more runs in English first-class cricket. His career aggregate is likely to remain a Gloucestershire record. However, these bare statistics do not tell the full story of Wally Hammond's contribution to Gloucestershire. It was the classical and graceful manner in which he scored runs that left an indelible mark on the memory.

He was a gifted all-rounder, capable of bowling anything from brisk swing to off-spin or even leg-breaks. Even so, he gradually became more reluctant to turn his arm over, but in the opinion of Bob Wyatt he was a good enough bowler to have taken over a hundred wickets each season. Wally was also a marvellous fielder, excelling in the outfield in his youth, before developing into one of the game's finest slip fielders. His haul of 78 catches in 1928 is still a record.

Born in Kent to a military family, young Wally and his parents initially spent a nomadic life in Hong Kong and Malta. His father was killed in 1914, and his mother subsequently settled in Southsea, with Wally attending Portsmouth Grammar School. Later, he was sent to board at Cirencester Grammar School, where his abundant sporting talent quickly became evident,

and was confirmed by an innings of 365* in a house match. It prompted his headmaster to write to the Gloucestershire committee, recommending that they should give a trial to the tall, muscular teenager, and in 1920 Wally was duly invited to play in Club and Ground matches.

After impressing the County officials, the seventeen-year-old amateur was included to play against Lancashire and Leicestershire at Cheltenham, and duly impressed the Festival crowd with his fluent stroke-play and swift fielding. However, he had no birth or residential qualification to play for Gloucestershire, and Kent tried to reclaim him. The outcome was that Wally spent the next two years qualifying for the County, playing in friendlies and club cricket, helping with coaching at Clifton College and spending the winters playing football for Bristol Rovers.

After qualifying, Wally became the lynchpin of the Gloucestershire batting, although at first he was too impetuous in his approach. He knew he could play every shot in the book, and often threw away his wicket by being too audacious.

Despite the odd rush of blood, Wally showed several flashes of true genius in the early 1920s, and his first great innings came in 1924 against Middlesex at Bristol. In their first innings Gloucestershire had been humbled for 31, but Wally then amazed with an unbeaten 174 that steered his side to a famous victory.

In August 1925, Wally also made a memorable 250* against Lancashire at Old Trafford and all

amassing a club record 2,860 runs, and establishing a new third-wicket partnership by adding 336 with Bev Lyon against Leicestershire. 1934 saw Wally pass two thousand again, and average 126 in Championship games. In 1936, he recorded his best county score – 317 v. Nottinghamshire.

In 1938, Wally became an amateur, and was duly appointed England captain for the Ashes series. He responded with 240 at Lord's, dominating the Australian attack with an innings of regal authority. During the winter, Wally led the England side to South Africa, before returning to the UK and leading Gloucestershire in the Championship in 1939.

After serving with the RAF, and playing in the 'Victory Tests' against Australia in 1945, Wally enjoyed leading Gloucestershire in 1946. He averaged 108 in Championship cricket, and at the end of the summer was appointed captain of the winter tour party to Australia.

It was in Australia that Wally began contemplating his cricketing future. He informed Gloucestershire that he intended to resign the captaincy and retire from the first-class game. On his return, he went into business, and only appeared once more for the County, against Somerset in 1951 as part of a membership drive. It was an unsuccessful return, and a sad way for a great player to end his career.

This diamond was not without flaws, and in the words of his biographer, David Foot, 'his life was touched by genius on the cricket field, yet elsewhere it was strewn with failure – in business, in human relationships and in the relative obscurity of his later years.' Despite being fêted by hordes of sycophantic admirers, Wally was a deeply private and stubborn individual. He was also too sparing in his praise and encouragement of young players, many of whom would have benefitted from a gentle word of advice from this great batsman.

After retiring, Wally settled in South Africa and invested his life savings in the motor trade, but within a few years, he had lost all of his capital. In the autumn of 1959, he was appointed Sports Administrator at Natal University. In 1962, he briefly returned to aid Gloucestershire's membership drive. However, in 1965, he suffered a heart attack and died at his home in Durban.

against an attack regarded at the time to be the most potent in the country.

Fine innings such as these led to Wally's call-up by the England selectors for the 1925/26 tour of the West Indies. However, it was a tour that nearly cost Wally his life, as he contracted syphilis and returned to Britain for urgent medical attention. He remained in a nursing home for several months and missed all of the 1926 season. Thankfully, he recovered and returned to County cricket in 1927 with a vengeance, amassing over 1,000 runs in just twenty-two days in May. He finished the season with over 2,528 Championship runs, and won a place on the winter tour to South Africa, where he made his Test debut at Johannesburg.

The next summer, he scored 2,456 runs in the Championship, and also recorded career-best bowling figures of 9-23 against Worcestershire at Cheltenham, and finished the game with match figures of 15-128. The following winter, he visited Australia and enjoyed one of the finest visits ever made by an English batsman. Wally scored a record 905 runs in the Ashes series, with double hundreds at Sydney and Melbourne, plus scores of 119 and 177 in the Adelaide Test.

His outstanding feats led to claims that Wally was the world's finest batsman, and over the next few years, it was only the legendary Don Bradman that drew comparison with him. The pair came head-to-head on the infamous 1932/33 Bodyline tour, before Wally travelled on to New Zealand, where he hit a record 336* in the Test at Auckland – then the highest individual score in Test cricket. He continued in record-breaking vein the following summer,

Timothy Harold Coulter Hancock

RHB & RM, 1991-present

Born: 20 April 1972, Reading, Berkshire

Batting

M	I	NO	Runs	Av
150	262	16	6737	27.39
180	*166*	*5*	*3533*	*21.94*

50	100	ct/st
40	6	95
16	*1*	*58*

Bowling

Balls	Runs	Wkts	Av	5wl	10wM
2877	1658	44	37.68	-	-
1290	*1098*	*45*	*24.40*		

Best Performances

220* v Nottinghamshire at Trent Bridge, 1998
3-5 v Essex at Colchester, 1998
110 v Northamptonshire at Bristol, 2000
6-58 v Scotland at Bristol, 1997

Tim Hancock has emerged over the last few years as a fine top order batsman, equally at home in the longer or shorter form of the game. These talents, allied to a sharp cricket brain, have already seen his elevation to the vice-captaincy of the County club. If he maintains his consistency, he could soon press for international honours.

Hancock showed promise as a young cricketer and hockey player at St Edward's School, Oxford. His aggressive batting for Oxfordshire in 1990 led to a trial with Gloucestershire, and a contract for the following season. In 1991, he made his County debut, and for the next few seasons he occupied a berth in the County's middle-order. He showed himself to be particularly strong off his legs, as well as having a ferocious square cut and a liking for coming down the track to hit spinners back over the top.

In the early part of his career, 'Herbie' had the tendency to do the hard work and get settled, only to play a sloppy shot and lose his wicket. At times, it looked as if Hancock would join the list of promising youngsters to lose their way in the game. But to his credit, a combination of greater experience, the added responsibility of being vice-captain, and a move up the order to open, have all helped Hancock to realise his talents. The hard work, plus the wise words of coach

John Bracewell, bore fruit as Hancock enjoyed his best ever season in 1998, scoring 1,227 first-class runs. His tally included a career-best 220* against Nottinghamshire at Trent Bridge in the season's final game. He fully deserved his County cap at the end of the summer.

In 1999, Hancock had a new opening partner in the form of the wily Kim Barnett, the former Derbyshire batsman. They formed an effective pairing, and during the course of NatWest competition the pair shared three century partnerships. One of these was in the quarter-final against Glamorgan, where the pair added 142 in a rollicking stand. Hancock's contribution was an assertive 90, and he was deservedly Man of the Match. His efforts also saw the County to a comfortable win, and he top scored in the final of the competition with an aggressive 74 as Gloucestershire defeated neighbours Somerset.

A broken finger in the match against Zimbabwe interrupted his season in 2000, but he returned to the side for the NatWest quarter-final against Northamptonshire at Bristol and celebrated with a maiden one-day hundred, by smashing Graeme Swann high over long-on.

Hancock is a fine fielder, a great scamperer in the outfield, and a handy medium pace bowler, especially in one-day games. His nagging and accurate seamers made him the trump card in Mark Alleyne's attack – particularly in the 2000 NatWest Trophy final, where he returned figures of 10-1-34-2 as Gloucester-shire beat Warwick-shire to win their fourth successive final.

Ian Joseph Harvey
RHB & RM, 1999-present

Born: 10 April 1972, Wonthaggi, Victoria

Batting

M	I	NO	Runs	Av
32	48	3	1355	30.11
62	59	2	1457	25.56

50	100	ct/st		
5	3	24		
6	-	15		

Bowling

Balls	Runs	Wkts	Av	5wI	10wM
5035	2307	112	20.60	6	1
3029	1926	131	14.70		

Best Performances
130* v Middlesex at Lord's, 2001
6-19 v Sussex at Hove, 2000
92 v Worcestershire at Bristol, 2001
5-19 v Northamptonshire at Bristol, 2000

Ian Harvey has been one of the most successful international cricketers playing in England over the past few years, especially in one-day games. The hugely talented Australian also cemented a regular place in his country's one-day international team, and he is regarded as the finest exponent of the slower ball in world cricket. It is his ability to deceive opposing batsmen, and blitz their bowlers with a fusillade of powerful strokes, that has helped Harvey to win international honours, besides underpinning Gloucestershire's recent success in one-day cricket.

Since 1999, Harvey has been the ace up the sleeve of captain Mark Alleyne, and it is no coincidence that Harvey's arrival on the County's staff has seen Gloucestershire enjoy their most successful ever period in one-day cricket. At first, it looked as if Harvey would have an undistinguished County career, as he arrived in chilly Britain with a back niggle and met with little success in the opening Championship matches. But as the weather improved, so did Harvey's performances, with a maiden Championship hundred and some useful performances with bat and ball. This was especially true in the National League, where his 30 wickets made him the competition's leading wicket-taker.

The following summer, the Victorian all-rounder came up trumps during Gloucestershire's remarkable one-day treble. His bowling at the death was watertight, with his devastating yorkers deciding the outcome of several games, especially in the NatWest Trophy. Harvey began with four wickets against both Leicestershire and Northants in the

early rounds, and then, after missing the semi-final with Lancashire while on one-day duty for Australia, Harvey flew back to Britain to be part of the team that was to beat Warwickshire in the final.

Earlier in the summer, he had played some explosive innings in the Benson & Hedges Cup, especially in the quarter-final against Sussex at Hove. Harvey smashed 88 from 68 balls, and then produced a spell of 3-28, bowling with skill and precision to thwart the best efforts of the Sussex batsmen. A hamstring tweak meant that he missed the semi-final with Lancashire, but was fit to return for the final with Glamorgan. Harvey's skidding bounce with the new ball accounted for both of Glamorgan's openers in his first spell, and he then returned to give a masterclass on the art of variable pace with the old ball, adding a further three wickets to finish with 5-34 to become only the third bowler in the competition's history to take five wickets in the final.

The talented all-rounder made his first-class debut for Victoria in 1993/94, before attending the Australian Cricket Academy. He was in the Australian One-Day side to play South Africa, and took the wicket of Jonty Rhodes with his second ball in international cricket. Since 1997/98, Harvey has played in over 40 one-day internationals, and was a member of the side that won the triangular series with England and Pakistan in 2001.

Alastair James Hignell

RHB & LB, 1974-1983

Born: 4 September 1955, Cambridge

Batting

M	I	NO	Runs	Av
137	231	35	5678	28.96
128	114	19	2240	23.58

50	100	ct/st
31	7	117
6	-	56

Bowling

Balls	Runs	Wkts	Av	5wl	10wM
121	98	3	32.67	-	-
3	4	-	-		

Best Performances

149* v Northamptonshire at Bristol, 1979
2-13 v Sri Lankans at Bristol, 1981
85* v Northamptonshire at Bristol, 1977

Alastair Hignell was the most recent Gloucestershire cricketer to appear for England in rugby internationals. The doughty all-round sportsman won 14 caps at full-back for England, as well as winning cricket and rugby blues for Cambridge between 1975 and 1978, and leading Cambridge against Oxford. Ankle injuries forced him to give up his fine rugby career with Bristol and England, but he developed into a forthright, pugnacious batsman and a fine all-round fielder, taking sharp catches close to the wicket as well as being outstanding in the deep.

Educated at Denstone, Alastair made his Gloucestershire debut in 1974 and, as befitted a fine rugby player, he made an immediate impression as a swift fielder with a safe pair of hands. At the end of the summer, he went up to Fitzwilliam College, Cambridge and won his first rugby blue, playing both at scrum-half and full-back. His excellent form resulted in selection at full-back in England's party for their Australia tour, and on 31 May 1975, he made his international debut against Australia at Brisbane. On returning to the UK, he showed what a fine all-rounder he was by regaining his place in the Cambridge XI, to win his first cricket blue.

1976 was the coming of age for Hignell as a cricketer, and he greatly benefited from being promoted to open the batting for Cambridge. During the summer, he emerged as a belligerent and free-scoring batsman, recording his maiden centuries for the University and Gloucestershire, with 101 against Kent at Fenner's, plus a gritty 119 against the West Indian tourists at Bristol. In 1977, he led the university cricket and rugby teams, and won more rugby caps for England. He led the University again in 1978, hitting 108 and 145 in the match against Surrey. Yet, after coming down he had a wretched County season, averaging 9.5 in Championship games.

1979 was a much more profitable summer, and there was a clear sign that lady luck was on his side early in his innings against Yorkshire at Cheltenham, when he played a ball from Geoff Cope into his stumps without dislodging a bail. He later registered his maiden Championship century, and made a career best 149* against Northants at Bristol in the season's final match.

Knee and ankle injuries restricted appearances in 1980, but in May he registered another century, with an unbeaten 100 against Somerset at Taunton. He also shared in a partnership of 254 in three-and-a-half hours with Zaheer Abbas to save the game for Gloucestershire after their West Country neighbours forced the follow-on.

During the winter months, Alastair had started teaching history in Bristol, and in 1983 he retired and joined the staff at Sherborne School in Dorset. However, two years later, he left to become a broadcaster, initially with the BBC. After a spell with HTV West in Bristol, he has rejoined BBC Radio in London, covering international and club rugby. In 2000, he was diagnosed with multiple sclerosis. He has since raised awareness of, and funds for the treatment of this debilitating condition.

Born: 15 March 1877, Headington, Oxfordshire
Died: 20 November 1942, Stroud

Batting

M	I	NO	Runs	Av
200	347	44	4373	14.43
50	100	ct/st		
10	-	47		

Bowling

Balls	Runs	Wkts	Av	5wl	10wM
37196	16957	584	29.03	24	5

Best Performances
92 v Middlesex at Lord's, 1906
9-34 v Sussex at Bristol, 1934

Harry Huggins was a clever medium pace bowler who was an admirable foil to the left-arm spin of George Dennett in the years either side of the First World War, and was a key weapon in the Gloucestershire attack.

In his early days with both Stroud CC and Gloucestershire, Huggins was a fast-medium bowler, who could make the ball swerve quite alarmingly in the air and skid off the surface. On occasions, his bowling could be rather wayward, and, later in his career, Huggins became quite expensive, with a few wags suggesting that this followed a good night's drinking. But the truth was that Huggins' waywardness stemmed from him trying too hard, especially when conditions did not favour any movement in the air.

However, on his day Huggins could be almost unplayable, and in May 1902, against Sussex at Hove, Huggins had the remarkable figures of 21.5-15-17-7 as he fully exploited a drying wicket. A couple of months later, he took 7-37 in 21.1 overs at Worcester as the home batsmen dramatically collapsed, only to be saved from defeat by rain on the final day.

The finest bowling performance of Huggins' career came at Bristol over the August Bank Holiday of 1904. Once again, Sussex were the

opponents as Huggins returned the figures of 9-34, and a measure of his effective combination of swerve and pace off the wicket can be gauged from the fact that eight of his wickets were clean bowled. C.B. Fry was one of the Sussex batsmen to be dismissed in both innings by Huggins, whom he described as 'equal to any bowler Sussex played against that summer'.

After putting on weight, Huggins became more of an off-cutter, concentrating on length and spin, as opposed to pace and swerve. As he got older and heavier, he lost his nip off the wicket, but the switch to off cutters allowed him to extended his County career after the war.

Huggins was also a hard hitting lower order batsman, who at one stage in his career looked like becoming an all-rounder. After some lusty innings as a tail-ender, Huggins moved up the order in 1904, hitting 53 at number eight against Nottinghamshire at Trent Bridge, as Gloucestershire recorded a mammoth 636. In 1906, he recorded a career-best 92 against Middlesex at Lord's, but by this time Huggins was back at number ten in the order, and his role with the bat was limited to a few lusty tail-end cameos, in addition to occasional duty as the County's nightwatchman.

After retiring from Championship cricket in 1921, Huggins acted as the County's scorer for a few seasons. He also continued to play club cricket for Stroud CC and in his later years belied his ample girth and receding hairline by playing a number of forcing innings.

Gilbert Laird Jessop

RHB & RFM, 1894-1914

Born: 9 May 1874, Cheltenham
Died: 11 May 1955, Fordington, Dorset

Batting

M	I	NO	Runs	Av
345	605	23	18936	32.53

50	100	ct/st		
93	36	357		

Bowling

Balls	Runs	Wkts	Av	5wl	10wM
30266	13853	620	22.34	30	3

Best Performances

286 v Sussex at Brighton, 1903
8-29 v Essex at Cheltenham, 1900

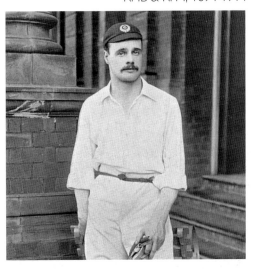

'No man has ever driven a cricket ball so hard, so high and so often in so many different directions. No man has ever made cricket so dramatic an entertainment.' So wrote C.B. Fry about Gilbert Jessop, who in the twenty years before the First World War was the most explosive and feared batsman in the country, and one of the most powerful hitters the game has ever seen.

In 1903, against Sussex at Hove, Jessop scored 200 in just two hours, whilst in 1905 at Bristol he smashed a double century in two hours and ten minutes against Somerset. However, his finest innings came at The Oval in 1902 against Australia as England were chasing 263 on a wet and spiteful wicket. They had already collapsed to 48-5 when Jessop strode to the wicket, but he then turned the game around completely with a quite brilliant and astounding century – in just 75 minutes – to see his side home to a memorable victory by just one wicket and put his name amongst the list of the game's immortals.

Jessop was certainly not a slogger who enjoyed the odd purple patch of form. If he had been, he would not enjoyed such a lengthy Test career from 1988 to 1912, nor would he have had such a productive association with Gloucestershire with over 18,000 runs and 36 centuries, six of which were against Yorkshire, regarded as having the finest attack in the country.

Indeed, in 1897 he hit his maiden century for Gloucestershire against the touring Philadelphians, whose attack included King and Clark, two of the leading bowlers in the first-class game. Three days later, he scored 126 in just 95 minutes against Warwickshire at Edgbaston, and his fusillade of blows so pleased W.G. that the good doctor leapt to his feet on the veranda of the pavilion, clapped loudly and yelled 'Well hit, Gilbert.' Jessop finished the season with over 1,200 runs and 116 wickets and was deservedly nominated as one of *Wisden*'s Five Cricketers of the Year.

After leaving Cambridge University in 1900, Jessop briefly worked on the Stock Exchange in London, but the departure of W.G. from Gloucestershire resulted in Jessop receiving the offer of leading the County. He duly accepted and returned to the West Country to become their captain and the most dynamic personality in the club over the next fifteen years, passing 1,000 runs in every season.

In 1900, he scored 2,210 runs, followed in 1901 by 2,323 runs, including 233 in two and a half hours for an England XI against Yorkshire at Lord's. In 1904, Jessop hit 206 in two and a half hours for Gloucestershire, against Nottinghamshire at Trent Bridge. Then, in 1907, he struck 240 out of 337 in 200 minutes against Sussex at Bristol, as well as 191 in an hour and a half for the Gentlemen of the South against the Players of the South at Hastings.

On top of this, he also produced some fine bowling performances, including 8-29 against Essex in 1900 and 8-58 against Middlesex in 1902. In addition, Jessop gave many exhilarating

or pulls making it very difficult for any bowler to contain him.

Before 1907, only hits completely out of the ground were worth six runs, so anything that cleared the playing area was accorded just four runs, not six as at present – had the rule for boundary hits been changed earlier, Jessop's hurricane blows would have been worth even more. However, what really makes Jessop's feats even more remarkable is that he had no formal coaching. He was self-taught, and unlike other Gloucestershire greats, had no headmaster or parent to push him, or influential acquaintances who could put in a good word in the ear of a committee man – instead, he did it all himself.

The son of a Cheltenham surgeon, he attended Cheltenham Grammar School, where his bowling prowess, rather than batting feats, won him his cricket colours at the tender age of thirteen. Indeed, he was so fast that apparently at the age of twelve he broke a man's wrist with one of his fast deliveries. The sudden death of his father meant that Gilbert had to leave school at the age of sixteen and earn his own living. He opted to go into teaching, and worked in Worcestershire and Essex, before moving nearer home to a job at Burford Grammar School. He also played with distinction for the Witney Town club and was invited to play for the Oxfordshire Colts, but he declined, as his goal was to play for Gloucestershire. The following year, he duly achieved this by making his County debut against Lancashire at Old Trafford. It looked though as if it might be an inauspicious debut as the youngster arrived at the wicket needing to prevent a hat-trick. But he was not overawed and calmly hit his first ball to the boundary fence.

In 1895, Jessop secured a post at Beccles College in Suffolk, where he scored 1,058 runs at an average of 132, and took 100 wickets at just 2.4 runs apiece. After another summer of County cricket with Gloucestershire, he then went up to Christ's College, Cambridge to read Classics, with the intention of being ordained for the Church. However, he met with more success on the sporting fields than in the examination room, and left Cambridge without a degree. How different things might have been for both Gloucestershire and England had Jessop secured a degree and entered the Church.

displays in the field with a fast and accurate throw, whilst his gathering and return of the ball was the finest, and nearest to perfection that contemporaries had seen. He excelled at cover-point before moving to mid-off, and it was a foolish batsman who ever attempt to steal a single wherever Jessop was standing.

The short and stocky batsman had first appeared for the County in 1894 as a fast and combative bowler who was a dangerous, yet erratic batsman with a good eye. Everything changed in 1897 with a century in just 40 minutes against Yorkshire at Harrogate. It followed a change in his grip to lower on the handle, allowing him to gain greater control and he become a ferocious hitter of the ball, utilising his great assets of a marvellous eye, quicksilver reflexes, strong shoulders and long arms. As he shaped to play the ball he bent low, earning him the title 'The Croucher'; after sighting the ball early, he would dance down the pitch to drive the swiftest bowling in the land. If the bowlers dropped short, Jessop would unleash powerful cuts

Roger David Verdon Knight

LHB & RM, 1971-1975

Born: 6 September 1946, Streatham, London

Batting

M	I	NO	Runs	Av
105	186	13	5610	32.42
102	*100*	*8*	*2086*	*22.67*

50	100	ct/st
29	11	93
13	*-*	*29*

Bowling

Balls	Runs	Wkts	Av	5wI	10wM
7096	3561	100	35.61	1	-
4548	*3130*	*112*	*27.95*		

Best Performances

144 v Glamorgan at Swansea, 1974
6-44 v Northamptonshire at Northampton, 1974
96 v Worcestershire at Worcester, 1975
5-39 v Surrey at Bristol, 1971

Roger Knight was a key member of the Gloucestershire side that won the Gillette Cup in 1973. The tall all-rounder had first played with modest success with Surrey, but during his five year career with Gloucestershire, Knight hit eleven centuries and won five Man of the Match awards, including two in 1973 as the County celebrated their first ever one-day trophy.

Educated at Dulwich College and Cambridge University, Knight began his County career with Surrey, before joining Gloucestershire in 1971. He had an immediate impact in his first season, scoring over 1,200 Championship runs and establishing himself as an effective number three in the order. After Mike Procter, Knight was their most successful and dependable batsman, showing a particular liking for getting onto the front foot and attacking the bowling in a stylish and classical fashion.

He also had a significant impact in the limited-overs games, with his accurate right-arm medium-pace bowling enhancing the resources at Tony Brown's disposal. During their Gillette Cup campaign of 1971, Knight delivered many important spells, in particular in the quarter-final against Surrey at Bristol, where he transformed the game with an inspired spell of five wickets for just one run in the space of ten balls. Knight finished with an analysis of 5-39 and

with Gloucestershire winning by 15 runs, he was Harold Gimblett's choice as Man of the Match.

In 1973, Knight picked up two further awards in the competition, beginning at Cardiff with an elegant 75, plus two wickets. Then, in the third round at Chelmsford, he had a fine all-round game with a forceful innings of 60, two fine catches and three wickets as Essex were defeated by 30 runs. Gloucestershire duly reached the final of the Gillette Cup, and Knight capped a fine season with 4-47 to help mop up the Sussex resistance and leave Gloucestershire celebrating their first major success since 1877.

He was viewed by some as a potential successor to Tony Brown as Gloucestershire's captain, but in 1975 Knight was appointed to a teaching post at Eastbourne College and he left to join Sussex. In 1978, he returned to The Oval, where he took over and transformed a struggling Surrey side. In five years at the helm, they went from languishing at the foot of the Championship table to four one-day finals at Lord's.

After retiring in 1984, Knight concentrated on his teaching career, during which time he ran a house and the cricket XI at Cranleigh, before becoming headmaster of Worksop College in 1990. Four years later, his talents in leadership and administration were transferred from the world of education to cricket, with his appointment as secretary of the MCC.

Born: 11 May 1919, Paddington, London
Died: 30 October 1991, Bristol

Batting

M	I	NO	Runs	Av
334	480	61	6288	15.00
50	**100**	**ct/st**		
21	1	189		

Bowling

Balls	Runs	Wkts	Av	5wI	10wM
52357	25831	908	28.44	37	5

Best Performances
100* v Worcestershire at Worcester, 1955
8-35 v Yorkshire at Bristol, 1956

George Lambert was the consummate team man, leading Gloucestershire's seam attack with great effect in the 1940s and 1950s. He bowled with the same sense of purpose and expectation irrespective of whether it was the first or last hour of the day's play – and all despite having to bowl on slow, low wickets at Bristol or on dry surfaces elsewhere, tailor-made for the Gloucestershire spinners.

For George, it was never a case of just having a couple of overs at the start of the innings, merely to take the shine off the ball before the slow bowlers went to work. Instead, he always bowled his heart out for his adopted County, taking over 900 wickets during his fourteen-year career, and many people consider the genial seamer to have been unlucky not to win international honours.

George was born and bred in London, and on leaving school he joined the MCC groundstaff. With few chances likely at Middlesex, the ebullient Cockney agreed to join Gloucestershire. After spending two years qualifying, he made his first-class debut in 1938. He subsequently formed a most potent and penetrative new ball partnership with Colin Scott. They complemented each other to the full, with Scott's brisk pace and Lambert's late in-swing acting as the perfect foil. The County had lacked such a pairing for so long, and as the two bowlers

enjoyed a profitable season in 1939, there was plenty of talk around the County Ground that one day the young tyros might play Test cricket. But the outbreak of war then robbed the two Gloucestershire men of six years of County cricket, and instead of furthering his cricket career in the 1940s, Lambert became a sergeant in the Army.

The loss of so many opportunities at such a formative time proved a stumbling block for many young cricketers whose careers were permanently blighted. This was not the case with George, although contemporaries believed he would have come closer to winning Test honours had he not spent so many years at war. He returned to County cricket in 1946, and immediately picked up where he had left off, bowling with spirit and purpose. But whilst George remained an effective and loyal workhorse, his new ball partner had lost his raw pace, and for a while Scott even experimented with spin. Their new ball partnership, which had been so effective before the war, was sadly a thing of the past.

George was a powerfully-built man with a classically smooth and copybook action. He was always willing to bowl, whatever the situation, and cheerfully kept a smile on his face even after working hard to keep the shine on the ball, only to see the spinners at the other end rub the ball in the dirt! Indeed, his career tally might have gone past a thousand had George not been withdrawn from the attack to allow Goddard and Cook to twirl away in tandem.

Thomas Langdon
RHB & SLA, 1900-1914

Born: 8 January 1879, Brighton, Sussex
Died: 30 November 1944, Nuneaton

Batting

M	I	NO	Runs	Av
279	513	14	10621	21.28

50	100	ct/st
57	6	204/3

Bowling

Balls	Runs	Wkts	Av	5wI	10wM
1264	835	19	43.94	-	-

Best Performances
156 v Surrey at the Oval, 1910
2-8 v Middlesex at Bristol, 1907

Tom Langdon was a solid right-handed batsman who was, alongside Gilbert Jessop, the mainstay in the Gloucestershire batting in the years leading up to the First World War. Their consistent run scoring often held together the County's batting at a time when the side languished in the lower part of the County table.

The most productive period of his career spanned the 1907 and 1908 seasons, when Gloucestershire recorded 16 Championship victories. Without Langdon's steady batting, the County might have sunk to the bottom of the table. In 1907, Langdon scored 1219 runs, without a century, and his consistency, allied to Jessop's magnificent strokeplay, was one reason behind the club's purple patch of form.

His finest hour during the 1907 season came in the match against the South African tourists. In the Gloucestershire first innings he shared a breezy opening partnership of 95 in barely an hour with Jack Board. Then, in their second innings, he carried his bat for 78, as all the other county's batsmen struggled against the Springbok bowlers. After Langdon's 78*, the next highest score in Gloucestershire's total of 151 was Gilbert Jessop with 20.

When Langdon joined the Gloucestershire staff in 1900, he was considered to be more of a bowler who could bat. Indeed, in his first appearance for Gloucestershire, against the 1900 West Indians at Bristol, Langdon took 3-57 and batted at number nine. But despite his lowly position,

the twenty-one year old showed his rich promise as a batsman with a quickfire half-century.

A month later, Langdon made his Championship debut with a stylish unbeaten 76 against Sussex at Bristol. Once again, he went in at number nine, and had he gone in earlier, he might even have recorded a maiden century in his first Championship appearance.

Gilbert Jessop, the County's captain, was highly impressed, both by Langdon's style and spirit, so in 1901, he promoted the young professional up the batting order to number three, and in only his second match in his new position, Langdon duly hit his maiden century, with an unbeaten 114 against Derbyshire at Bristol.

In the course of the next decade, Langdon added a further five hundreds, including 140 against Sussex at Gloucester in 1913, and 156 against Surrey at The Oval in 1910. However, Langdon enjoyed a fair share of good luck during this career best innings, twice playing onto the stumps, only to see, with relief, the bails not fall.

His opening partnership with Jack Board helped lay the foundations of several sizeable totals, and Langdon developed into the reliable, sheet anchor of the Gloucestershire side. He was also a fine fielder, both in the deep and close to the wicket, and he sometimes took over behind the stumps when Jack Board was injured or unavailable.

David Valentine Lawrence

RHB & RF, 1981-1997

Born: 28 January 1964, Gloucester

Batting

M	I	NO	Runs	Av
170	198	37	1720	10.68
108	45	19	284	10.92

50	100	ct/st
2	-	44
-	-	24

Bowling

Balls	Runs	Wkts	Av	5wI	10wM
24100	14919	477	31.27	19	1
5152	3928	147	26.72		

Best Performances

66 v Glamorgan at Abergavenny, 1991
7-47 v Surrey at Cheltenham, 1988
38* v Yorkshire at Scarborough, 1991
6-20 v Combined Universities at Bristol, 1991

David Lawrence will be largely remembered as the burly fast bowler whose promising Test career with England was dramatically ended by a horrific injury. His left kneecap split apart and dislocated, just as he was running in to bowl during the Third Test against New Zealand at the Basin Reserve Ground in Wellington on 10 February 1992.

As always, Lawrence was running in with great purpose, but that day he was striving even harder after being told by his County colleague Jack Russell that the ball was not hitting his gloves as firmly as normal. Lawrence later recalled, 'I thought, I'll show him, and I ran in for the next over as hard as I could, but as I bowled, I felt a pain like I had never experienced before. It was as if someone had just shot me through the back of the knee. I remained conscious through the whole thing, although I wished that I had passed out ...'

Born in Gloucester of Jamaican parents, Lawrence was the first English-born non-white cricketer to represent both Gloucestershire and England, as well as being the first English Test cricketer to list break-dancing as his main recreation! A popular and wholehearted competitor, Lawrence was capable of bowling with extreme pace and hostility, and when he got his 'radar' right, his raw pace worried the finest of batsmen.

He made his County debut in 1981 as a seventeen year old, and in his early years 'Syd' was prone to bowling too short, or being erratic in line and length. But as he matured, his accuracy improved, and his greater control was rewarded with a regular place in the County side, and he formed a potent new-ball partnership with Courtney Walsh. Bowling in tandem with the great West Indian helped 'Syd' to further improve his game. In 1985, he took 85 first-class wickets to win both the Cricket Writers Club Award as the Young Player of the Year and a place on the England B winter tour to Sri Lanka. Lawrence made his Test debut in 1988 against Sri Lanka at Lord's, and won selection for the winter tour to India.

The tour was subsequently cancelled and 'Syd' had to wait until 1991 to reappear in Test cricket, playing twice against the West Indians, and then against the Sri Lankans to win selection for the fateful tour to New Zealand. He began the series with a five-wicket haul, and broke Trevor Franklin's arm at Napier, before suffering the awful injury a week after his twenty-eighth birthday.

In all, Lawrence won five Test caps, and he would certainly have won many more had injury not struck, robbing both County and country of a genuine fast bowler, as well as a most engaging and larger than life character. As befitted a fitness fanatic, Lawrence bravely made attempts to return to the County game, but he snapped his kneecap again in the gym. After further treatment, Lawrence played again in 1997, but he was thwarted by further injury and retired at the end of the season. He now has business interests in Bristol, and has worked as a summariser on BBC Radio.

Jonathan Lewis
RHB & RM, 1995-present

Born: 26 August 1975, Aylesbury

Batting

M	I	NO	Runs	Av
81	122	24	1176	12.00
83	50	22	305	10.89

50	100	ct/st
-	-	16
-	-	17

Bowling

Balls	Runs	Wkts	Av	5wI	10wM
14512	7248	282	25.70	13	1
3708	2824	96	29.42		

Best Performances
62 v Worcestershire at Cheltenham, 1999
8-95 v Zimbabweans at Gloucester, 2000
33* v Somerset at Bristol, 1998
4-23 v Durham at Bristol, 2001

Jon Lewis is one of the new generation of fine County bowlers, and in 2000 was the country's leading first-class wicket-taker amongst English-qualified bowlers, with 72 wickets at 20 apiece. Lewis made his Minor County debut for Wiltshire in 1993, before joining the Northamptonshire staff in 1994. However, after one season in the East Midlands, he left without having played any first-team cricket and joined Gloucestershire for 1995. It proved to be a shrewd move, as he won a place in the Westcountry side by the end of the summer.

Lewis' accuracy and confidence had impressed the County's coaching staff, and although the youngster had no great pace, he showed an ability to move the ball and surprise batsmen with extra bounce. Lewis also benefited from bowling at the other end to the great Courtney Walsh, and then in a fine new-ball partnership with Mike Smith.

His partnership with Smith began in 1997, when Lewis made strong headway during the summer to finish with 54 first-class wickets. The following year, Lewis reverted back to first change, and had the benefit of bowling after Walsh and Smith had made early inroads with the new ball. He started the season with a spell of 6-11 in 38 balls against Glamorgan, and ended with a commendable haul of 59 first-class wickets as well as his County cap.

Lewis has continued to flourish under coach John Bracewell and captain Mark Alleyne, and with their wise advice and encouragement, Lewis finished one short of another haul of fifty wickets in 1999. The highlight of the summer on an individual basis were career-best figures of 7-56 against Nottinghamshire at Bristol, and his first ten-wicket match haul saw Gloucestershire to a fine victory. On a collective level, Lewis was delighted to be part of the Gloucestershire squad that won the Benson & Hedges Super Cup and the NatWest Trophy. Although he missed out on playing in the latter final, Lewis was in the team for the Super Cup final against Yorkshire at Lord's, and his figures of 3-32 reflected not only his own confidence in bowling in one-day games, but that of all of Alleyne's men.

Lewis went from strength to strength in 2000, especially in Championship cricket, and after advice from coach John Bracewell, he modified his grip to more over the top of the ball. This allowed him to hit the pitch much harder, and adjust his length so he was bowling just short of a good length. He reaped the rewards in a vintage season in Championship cricket, with a tally of 72 first-class wickets – more than any other bowler, except for Worcestershire's Glenn McGrath – which helped him to become the County's Player of the Year.

He had a good start to the 2001 season, with an impressive, match-winning return of 10-1-13-3 in the Benson & Hedges Cup match against Northamptonshire at Bristol. Then in the quarter-final against Durham, Lewis returned figures of 4-23 from 10 hostile overs. He played little after being injured, but a return to form in 2002 should see him continue his quest for international recognition.

Beverley Hamilton Lyon

RHB & OB, 1921-1947

Born: 19 January 1902, Caterham, Surrey
Died: 22 June 1970, Balcombe, Sussex

Batting

M	I	NO	Runs	Av
238	395	20	9550	25.46
50	100	ct/st		
43	15	246		

Bowling

Balls	Runs	Wkts	Av	5wI	10wM
3396	2218	50	44.36	1	-

Best Performances
189 v Surrey at Cheltenham, 1934
5-72 v Yorkshire at Bristol, 1937

Bev Lyon, Gloucestershire's skipper from 1929 to 1934, was widely regarded as one of the most astute captains of his generation, always prepared to risk defeat if there was any hope of victory.

After taking over from Harry Rowlands, he helped to transform Gloucestershire's fortunes. In his first year in charge, they won fifteen Championship matches, made a bid for the County title and defeated the 1929 South Africans. The following year they tied with the Australians and won fifteen Championship fixtures.

Lyon was a devout believer in playing attractive cricket, but, like other progressive-thinking captains, he fell foul of the authorities after what was viewed as 'rule bending' in the rain-affected match with Yorkshire in 1931. The two teams had sat in the Sheffield pavilion for two days, with Lyon rummaging through various books on the laws of the game, trying to see how his team might secure the fifteen points for a win.

Under the regulations of the time, fifteen points were only possible in a two-innings match, so when the third day dawned, it seemed that the two Counties would settle for a one-innings match and just five points for a first innings lead. But Lyon approached Frank Greenwood to suggest that each side should bowl four byes before declaring, thereby getting their first innings out of the way, so that they could play instead for fifteen points. Greenwood agreed, but in pursuit of 172 in two and a half hours, his side were dismissed for 124 – their only defeat that season.

Lyon's clever plan had paid off, but the mandarins within the MCC were upset by his ploy and they later revised the regulations to outlaw what they considered to be illegal declarations. Lyon became increasingly frustrated by the negative outlook of some County captains, who shied away from setting exciting declarations. It was no coincidence that Lyon put business before cricket during 1932, prior to standing down as captain in 1934. He then played infrequently, making a final appearance for the West at the 1948 Kingston Festival.

Educated at Rugby and Oxford, Lyon won blues in 1922 and 1923, and developed into a dashing stroke-maker for Gloucestershire, passing a thousand runs on four occasions. He missed the 1925 season when on business in India, and in 1928 struck his maiden century during a stand of 285 with Wally Hammond as the Surrey attack were taken apart at 80 runs an hour. The captaincy made Lyon into a responsible batsman, and in 1929 he scored three centuries, followed by five in 1930, including a hundred in each innings against Essex at Bristol.

Lyon was also a brave fielder close to the wicket, taking many sharp catches at short-leg or in the slips off the bowling of Parker and Goddard. Both of these great spinners received constant encouragement from Lyon to keep throwing the ball up, so that a batsman would eventually miscue the spinning ball. When the mistake came, he would shout 'That's out', before sitting down on the turf, and applauding as the catch was taken.

Barrie John Meyer
RHB & WK, 1957-1971

Born: 21 August 1932, Bournemouth

Batting

M	I	NO	Runs	Av
406	569	191	5371	14.20
44	*25*	*5*	*134*	*6.70*

50	100	ct/st
11	-	708/119
-	-	*47/5*

Bowling

Balls	Runs	Wkts	Av	5wI	10wM
30	28	0	-	-	-

Best Performances

63 v Indians at Cheltenham, 1959
63 v Oxford University at Bristol, 1962
63 v Sussex at Bristol, 1964
21 v Middlesex at Bristol, 1963

By his own admission, Barrie Meyer never expected to become a County cricketer, never mind a wicketkeeper and a Test match umpire. When he was growing up in Bournemouth, it seemed that if the talented youngster was going to have a career in sport, it would be as a footballer. Whilst he showed promise as a hard-hitting batsman and fast bowler at Boscombe School, young Barrie really shone at football, and the inside forward won selection for the Hampshire Schools team and the English Association of Boys Clubs side against their Welsh counterparts at Wrexham. The Bournemouth club showed a passing interest in him, but the seventeen-year-old Meyer secured a trial instead with Bristol Rovers, and the following year he made his League debut.

After completing National Service, he rejoined the Bristol Rovers staff, and like many young footballers, he decided to keep fit during the summer by playing cricket and working on the groundstaff at the County Ground. During his National Service, Barrie had played cricket for an Army team, and when they were short, he volunteered to keep wicket. He enjoyed being behind the stumps, and proved a natural gloveman. By working at the County Ground, he got the chance to play in Second XI, plus club and ground matches. Some impressive innings and neat displays behind the stumps led to him being offered a contract with the County club.

In 1955, he joined the Gloucestershire staff, primarily as a reserve batsman, as there were already three other 'keepers on the County's books – Andy Wilson, Peter Rochford and Bobby Etheridge. Within a couple years, though, Wilson had retired, while Rochford had also left the club, so when Etheridge decided to tour Germany in spring 1958 with Bristol City FC, Meyer was given his chance behind the stumps. He proved such a success that he retained the post when Etheridge returned, and he remained the County's first-choice 'keeper up until 1971.

Meyer proved to be a very dependable 'keeper, going about his job without any fuss. Indeed, after establishing himself as the County's 'keeper in 1958, it was not until 1967 that he missed his first game, and in 1962 he equalled the club record by taking six catches in an innings against Somerset at Taunton. He continued to play League football during the winter months, scoring 60 goals in 139 appearances for Bristol Rovers, and playing for Plymouth Argyle, Newport County and Bristol City. After hanging up his football boots, Barrie spent several winters playing cricket and coaching in South Africa.

After retiring in 1972, he joined the first-class umpires list, and soon became one of the most respected officials, standing in the 1979 and 1983 World Cup Finals, 23 limited-overs Internationals and 26 Tests between 1978 and 1993. He retired as an umpire at the end of the 1997 season, shortly after his sixty-fifth birthday and following a lifetime in professional sport.

William Evans Midwinter

RHB & RM, 1877-1882

Born: 19 June 1851, Lower Meend, St Briavels
Died: 3 December 1890, Yarra Bend, Melbourne

Batting

M	I	NO	Runs	Av
58	88	8	1605	20.06
50	100	ct/st		
5	2	52		

Bowling

Balls	Runs	Wkts	Av	5wI	10wM
12914	3672	231	15.89	17	2

Best Performances

107* v Somerset at Gloucester, 1882
7-27 v Yorkshire at Sheffield, 1881

Billy Midwinter has the unique distinction of being the only person to have ever played for England against Australia as well as for Australia against England. He will also be remembered as the person who in 1878 was at the centre of a County or country row that saw 'W.G.' at loggerheads with the management of the Australian tour.

Born in the Forest of Dean, his family emigrated to Australia when Billy was nine. He made his first-class debut in 1874/75, followed two years later by his Test debut for Australia. In 1887, he agreed to join Gloucestershire, and he marked his first season with a fine bowling performance in their victory over an England side, returning match figures of 11-81. At the end of 1877, Billy headed back to Australia, on the understanding that he would return to play for Gloucestershire the following summer. However, after another fine season with Victoria, Billy was selected by Australia for the tour to England, and soon after arriving back on British soil, W.G. contacted Billy saying that he was wanted for Gloucestershire's opening Championship match of season against Surrey at the Oval.

In the interim, Billy had been promised highly lucrative benefit matches in Melbourne and Sydney if he threw his lot in with the Australians, so he opted to remain with the tourists for their match against Middlesex at Lord's. W.G. was furious after arriving at The Oval to find that Billy had not turned up, and his mood did not improve when Australian officials arrived at the ground to tell W.G. about Billy's change of allegiance. With his close friend 'Frizzie' Bush, W.G. then took a cab over to St John's Wood, where he stormed into the visitors' dressing room. After a chat with the all-rounder, the doctor won the day, and returned with Billy to The Oval. In the end, Midwinter scored just 4 and 0, as Gloucestershire lost their first match for two years, but he remained with the County for the rest of season as the Australians toured England a man short, and nearly withdrew from their fixture with Gloucestershire.

He proceeded to have a couple of quite productive seasons with Gloucestershire, and in 1881/82 he toured Australia with the England side. However, there were still uncertainties as to whether he would remain loyal to the England side and, as one contemporary said, 'one day he is an Australian and the next he is English'. Little surprise then that in 1882 he changed his allegiances back to Australia and ended his connections with Gloucestershire. He subsequently toured England in 1884 with Australia, before health problems forced him to retire in 1886.

Billy moved into the hotel trade, but shortly afterwards was hit by three tragedies. Firstly, his ten-month-old daughter died of pneumonia, then his wife died of apoplexy, and three months later his son also died. Heartbroken and ill-tempered, Billy was admitted to the Kew asylum in Melbourne, where he was diagnosed as showing signs of insanity. By September 1890, Billy was paralysed from the waist down and prone to bouts of unconsciousness, and in December he died in the asylum.

Percy Thomas Mills
RHB & RM/OB, 1902-1929

Born: 7 May 1879, Cheltenham
Died: 8 December 1950, Abingdon, Berkshire

Batting

M	I	NO	Runs	Av
346	546	116	5050	11.74

50	100	ct/st		
9	-	186		

Bowling

Balls	Runs	Wkts	Av	5wI	10wM
49280	20736	823	25.19	39	5

Best Performances
95 v Worcestershire at Worcester, 1923
7-30 v Derbyshire at Chesterfield, 1922

Percy Mills was another of the great characters of the Gloucestershire team who played either side of the First World War. Small in stature Mills may have been, but few of the County's players at the time had a bigger or warmer heart.

Like many fine off-spinners, Mills began his career at schoolboy and club level as a seam bowler, before converting to spin, and becoming the dependable and hard-working partner of the great Charlie Parker. Percy was also a doughty batsman, cheerfully volunteering to open the batting when the County were without their regular batsmen.

In the late 1920s, Mills also ran the club's cricket nursery at the Fry's ground in Bristol, where he acted as a kind and genial advisor to the County's young colts, quickly spotting any technical weaknesses, but taking great care not to stifle a youngster's enthusiasm. Throughout his distinguished career, Percy had been a fine role model for the younger players, cutting a dapper and neat figure off the field, always with a cheerful outlook, and willing to give a jolly word of encouragement to any young player who was down on his luck.

Percy joined the County in 1902, initially as a right-arm seam bowler. However, after a few seasons with the new ball, he decided to change styles and switched to slower off-cutters. His change certainly prolonged his career, and Percy's off-spin proved to be a wonderful foil to the left-arm spin of Parker. They contrasted each other in more than just bowling styles, with Parker being the quick-tempered radical, never afraid to ruffle a few feathers and ever ready to discuss political theory.

By contrast, Mills was a far more gentle soul, even to the extent of smiling at any fielders who might drop a catch off him.

Chalk and cheese they may have been, with characters and political views poles apart, but when bowling in tandem, Mills and Parker proved to be a fine combination. Their combined accuracy and success was such that on many occasions, the two spinners took the new ball, and then continued unchanged right through an innings. Sometimes there was no need for the Gloucestershire captain to even employ another bowler in the second innings, as the two spinners made light of the opposition batsmen. In fact, at Ashby-de-la-Zouch in 1922 the two bowled unchanged throughout the match with Leicestershire.

A few contemporary observers have written that the success of the combination stemmed from Percy's wonderful accuracy, keeping the batsmen contained at one end, whilst Parker took the wickets at the other. This may be a little uncharitable on the jovial Mills. In 1926, he took 101 wickets at just a shade over 23, and during his loyal career, he enjoyed many productive spells. One example was against Worcestershire in 1922, where Mills returned match figures of 9-43, as the Worcester batsmen were hustled out for 58 and 52 by the two Gloucestershire spinners to see their side to a comfortable innings victory.

Clement Arthur Milton

RHB & RM, 1948-1974

Born: 10 March 1928, Bedminster

Batting

M	I	NO	Runs	Av
585	1017	119	30218	33.65
55	*52*	*5*	*1095*	*23.30*

50	100	ct/st
52	152	718
5	*-*	*22*

Bowling

Balls	Runs	Wkts	Av	5wI	10wM
8316	3567	79	45.15	1	-
24	*26*	*2*	*13.00*		

Best Performances

170 v Sussex at Cheltenham, 1965
5-64 v Glamorgan at Gloucester, 1950
87 v Nottinghamshire at Trent Bridge, 1968
2-26 v Sussex at Arundel, 1972

Arthur Milton was the last man to represent England at both cricket and football, playing for England in their international against Austria at Wembley in 1951/52, and appearing in six Tests as a top order batsman. In his first Test, Milton celebrated his selection with an unbeaten century against the 1958 New Zealanders, and so became the first Gloucestershire player since the days of W.G. to make a hundred on his England debut.

In a County career that spanned four decades, Milton developed into a steady and accomplished batsman. He was a fine judge of a quick single and was a player who always appeared to have plenty of time to play his shots, especially off the back foot, and was particularly adept at pulling and cutting.

Milton was also an outstanding all-round fielder, and when he retired in 1974, his career haul of 718 catches was the highest for the County by a fielder. As befitted such a natural athlete with sharp reflexes, Milton was equally impressive in the slips, at short-leg or in the covers, fielding in each position with great agility and no little success either, winning the 'Brylcreem' fielding cup for the most number of catches in 1954 and 1956. He also equalled the world record by taking seven catches in a day against Sussex at Hove in

1952, and it was these attributes as a fielder that led to his selection as England's twelfth man during the 1953 Ashes series.

The all-rounder made his Gloucestershire debut in 1948 against Northamptonshire, and then hit a half-century against the Combined Services – an innings which helped to secure a contract with the County. For the next few summers, Milton played in their middle order and bowled gentle swingers, before moving up to open the batting in 1951, following an injury to Martin Young. This proved to be a turning point in his career, and his phlegmatic approach and fine technique allowed him to quickly settle into his new role, as he hit his maiden century against Somerset at Taunton and finished the summer with 1,364 Championship runs.

During the winter, Milton made his debut on the wing for Arsenal, and had an immediate impact, so much so that after just twelve impressive appearances for the Gunners, Milton won selection for the English side. His call-up came at a time when England were without the injured Tom Finney, whilst Stanley Matthews was out of favour, and although it was Milton's only England cap, it was recognition of his talents on the football field. In February 1955, Milton joined Bristol City, whom he helped to the Third Division title, before retiring at the end of the season, aged twenty-seven, to concentrate on his cricket career.

By this time, he had become a consistent run scorer, having topped the Gloucestershire averages in 1952 with 1,881 Championship runs, and after listening to sound advice from George Emmett, he became the County's regular opener from 1954. By 1956, Milton's consistency and fluent stroke-play had taken him to the fringe of the England team, playing for the MCC against Australia and appearing for The Rest against Surrey.

In November 1956, Milton broke a bone in his left wrist whilst playing in a charity football match. The injury took a long time to heal, forcing him to sit on the sidelines until July, by which time he had few chances to press his claims for inclusion in the Test side. It was a different story, however, in 1958, where some good form with Gloucestershire, and an injury to Colin Cowdrey saw Milton being put on standby for the Second Test against New Zealand.

The Kent batsman recovered in time to play, but Milton won selection in the Third Test and marked his inclusion with a debut hundred. Then, in the Gents v. Players match, Milton broke his nose whilst fielding at short-leg and had to miss the Fourth Test. Fortunately, he soon recovered and returned to the side for the final Test. He also won selection in the MCC party for the visit to Australia and New Zealand, in addition to being nominated as one of *Wisden*'s Five Cricketers of the Year.

Milton began the tour in good form, with a half-century against South Australia, followed by 116 against Victoria at Melbourne. This won him a place in the First and Third Tests, but in early January he badly damaged a finger whilst batting against Victoria at Melbourne, and subsequently had to return home.

He regained his fitness early in 1959 and enjoyed a prolific season with Martin Young – the pair amassed between them over 3, 500 runs and were responsible for 11 of Gloucestershire's 12 hundreds in the Championship. Milton's seven hundreds included 104 for the MCC against India, which saw Milton return to the England side for the first two games of the Test series.

However, the Second Test at Lord's proved to be Milton's final appearance in England colours, and despite being one of the country's most dependable openers and agile fielders, he was not called up again. Even so, Milton became the mainstay of the Gloucestershire batting and in 1967, at the age of

thirty-nine, he enjoyed his most productive season, scoring over two thousand runs before being appointed the County's captain for 1968. He had acted as their leader before when others were injured, most notably in 1961 when Tom Pugh broke his jaw. His season as the County's leader also saw Milton share in the County's record opening stand, adding 315 with David Green against Sussex at Hove. Later in the summer, he registered his fiftieth first-class hundred with a typically graceful century against the Australian tourists.

Despite having a shrewd cricket brain, Milton did not really enjoy the role of captain and he stood down from the post at the end of the season. In 1970, he announced his retirement, but the following year, he answered an SOS call to return to their injury-ravaged side and subsequently remained with the County until 1974.

RHB & WK, 1876-1887

Born: 14 November 1850, Shoreham-by-Sea
Died: 2 February 1914, Polurrian, Mullion

Batting

M	I	NO	Runs	Av
64	101	7	2072	22.04
50	100	ct/st		
9	3	45/15		

Bowling

Balls	Runs	Wkts	Av	5wI	10wM
-	-	-	-	-	-

Best Performances
121 v Somerset at Taunton, 1883

At one stage in the early 1870s it looked as if William Moberly would remain a talent unfilled on the cricket field, having failed to win a blue at Oxford after a promising schoolboy crickett career at Rugby.

He was also a fine rugby player and met with more success on the rugby pitches of Oxford than the cricket fields, winning a blue in 1873, as well as representing England against Scotland in 1872. After leaving Oxford, Moberley taught for a year in the Midlands, and also made a few appearances for Warwickshire and Leicestershire, before moving to the West Country in 1874 to take up a teaching position at Clifton College. He subsequently won a regular place in the Gloucestershire side in the second half of every season from 1876, and for the next twelve summers, he was, after the great W.G., one of the County's most reliable top order batsmen.

Moberly's finest performance was probably his 103 against Yorkshire in the famous match at Cheltenham in 1876 during which W.G. made 318* – a Gloucestershire record, and at the time the highest ever score in a County Championship match. Moberly and W.G. also shared a stand of 261 for the fifth wicket, with the two Gloucestershire amateurs mastering the powerful Yorkshire bowlers, and all on a wicket that on the second day had been freshened up by morning rain.

The following year, Moberly hit an unbeaten 101 against Nottinghamshire at Trent Bridge, and was in the County's side that defeated an England XI in a match at The Oval in aid of the Grace Testimonial Fund. For the man who had come so close to being a dark blue, this was a purple period indeed, and according to W.G., Moberly was 'from 1876 to 1881 one of the most brilliant batsmen in England, his large scores against first-class bowling being made in perfect style.'

Moberly's success was based on a good, quick eye and a very sound technique, the Sussex-born amateur rarely having to resort to hit the ball in the air. The square and late cuts were his most effective strokes, and in W.G.'s words 'you saw the flash of the bat when he made them, and a second or two afterwards the ball had reached the boundary.'

Moberly was also a fine and exuberant fielder, both in the deep and close to the wicket. On a couple of occasions, when his good friend 'Frizzie' Bush was indisposed, he capably filled in behind the stumps, and like everything he did on a cricket field, Moberly showed a most enthusiastic approach. He also had a successful academic career, running a house at Clifton from 1892, and then being appointed the school's deputy head in 1907, before retiring in 1913.

Clifford Ivon Monks

RHB & RM, 1935-1952

Born: 4 March 1912, Keynsham
Died: 23 January 1974, Coalpit Heath, Bristol

Batting

M	I	NO	Runs	Av
65	101	17	1589	18.91
50	100	ct/st		
7	1	32		

Bowling

Balls	Runs	Wkts	Av	5wl	10wM
2931	1629	36	45.25	-	-

Best Performances
120 v Cambridge University at Bristol, 1948
4-70 v Worcestershire at Worcester, 1963

Cliff Monks took one of the greatest catches in Gloucestershire's history, with his memorable feat coming against Middlesex at Cheltenham in mid-August 1947, at a time when the two Counties were in a neck-and-neck race for the Championship title.

Middlesex arrived at the College Ground without the services of Denis Compton and Jack Robertson, who were both playing for England against the South Africans at The Oval. Knowing that the outcome of the match was likely to determine the outcome of the Championship, a record crowd of 14,500 packed into the ground on the first day, and the gates had to be shut, leaving many disappointed supporters outside.

Middlesex had secured a slender lead of 27 in their first innings, but their top order struggled on the second morning against the wily Tom Goddard. Walter Robins, the Middlesex captain, then launched a fierce counter-attack, smashing 45 in 49 minutes, before attempting another huge legside hit off Goddard.

It looked like being a certain six, but Monks sprinted along the boundary rope from long-on and, despite many spectators having spilled onto the field, he took a stunning head high catch. Without any hesitation in his stride and with one hand outstretched in front of the enormous crowd, he almost plucked the ball from their midst. His miraculous catch brought a huge roar, and even Robins joined in with the congratulations, standing in the middle of the wicket and

clapping his bat in recognition of Monks' efforts.

The last six wickets fell for 16 runs, as Goddard returned the fine figures of 8-86. Gloucestershire were left to score 169 to win, but their batsmen struggled against the Middlesex spinners. Monks, batting at number six, was one of the wily Jack Young's five victims as Gloucestershire were dismissed for exactly 100. The 68-run victory gave the depleted Middlesex side the fillip they needed in the final fortnight of the season, whilst Gloucestershire could not regain the lost ground and they finished the season in runners-up spot, 20 points behind Middlesex.

Monks was a steady right-hand batsman and seam bowler, who had first played for the County as an amateur in 1935, before turning professional the following year. Like many of his generation, his best years were lost to the Second World War. After being demobbed in 1947, he never commanded a regular place in the side and only appeared in six Championship matches during the summer, but, as his stunning catch showed, he was still a fine fielder. Monks was a man of many talents, and after retiring in 1952, he had a successful life outside cricket as an artist, composer, stonemason, church organist and choirmaster.

John Brian Mortimore

RHB & OB, 1950-1975

Born: 14 May 1933, Southmead, Bristol

Batting

M	I	NO	Runs	Av
594	928	114	14917	18.32
93	68	21	494	10.51

50	100	ct/st		
61	4	320		
1	-	26		

Bowling

Balls	Runs	Wkts	Av	5wI	10wM
104876	38487	1696	22.69	72	8
3612	2273	78	29.14		

Best Performances

149 v Nottinghamshire at Trent Bridge, 1963
8-59 v Oxford University at The Parks, 1959
36 v Surrey at The Oval, 1964
4-12 v Glamorgan at Lydney, 1971

John Mortimore was, in the view of many long-standing supporters, the finest off-spinner Gloucestershire produced in the post-war era.

The son of an employee at Bristol's famous Wills factory, John was educated at Cotham Grammar School, where he received plenty of encouragement to take part in ball games. His first real coaching came in the Nevil Road nets, where, under the tutelage of George Emmett, the tall, slim youngster learnt how to impart as much spin as his young fingers would allow. Emmett also impressed upon him the need for accuracy in length and flight, as well as being prepared to bowl for hour after hour. All were invaluable lessons for Mortimore, who repaid his wise coach with 1,696 wickets in his twenty-six-year career.

He joined the County's staff shortly after leaving school at the age of sixteen, and after an impressive debut against the West Indians at Cheltenham, his name was pencilled in as a long-term replacement for Tom Goddard. The young apprentice got a chance to replace the old sorcerer far sooner than anyone expected, as Goddard was forced into retirement after contracting pneumonia.

In his first full season, Mortimore snaffled 48 wickets, but then had to do his National Service, and for the next two years, was attached to the Signals Regiment of the Army, based at Catterick Camp. Even so, he got the opportunity to play in Services cricket and continue his cricketing apprenticeship, before returning to Bristol a more mature bowler.

Indeed, in 1954, he took 69 Championship wickets to win his County cap. Over the next few years, he showed immaculate control, nagging away at the best batsmen, even on the most unhelpful of pitches, and forcing them to take risks against him in order to score. At the Cheltenham Festival of 1962, he had one of his finest spells for Gloucestershire, taking four wickets in five balls against Lancashire during a remarkable return of 13-9-9-5 as the visitors plummeted to an innings defeat.

By this time, Mortimore had also moved into the all-rounder category, having developed into a forceful lower order batsman, and in 1955 he scored a maiden hundred against Oxford University. In the early 1960s he moved up the order, sometimes even batting at number four, and in 1963 he scored his maiden Championship hundred against Nottinghamshire at Trent Bridge.

During the winter months, he had started working for Rediffision, before deciding to qualify as an accountant. However, in November 1958, he had other things to think about as he received an SOS from Australia to fly out to reinforce the MCC party. The call came as a complete surprise to the twenty-four year old, who had never been selected in any representative games. Despite not having picked up a bat or ball for almost two months, he flew out to Australia, where he joined his County colleagues Tom Graveney and Arthur Milton; it became the first time that three of the County's players had been on an official English tour.

Mortimore duly made his Test debut in the Fifth Test at Melbourne, and marked his England debut with the wicket of Alan Davidson, a sound innings of 44*and a share in a stubborn partnership of 63 with Fred Trueman. He played in two further Tests on the New Zealand leg of the tour, before returning home in the spring of 1959; in the summer that followed he became the first Gloucestershire player to perform the Double since Reg Sinfield in 1937. In all, he struck 1,060 runs and captured 113 wickets, including 8-57 against Oxford University.

He also won a further two caps in the Test series with India in 1959, yet despite being at the peak of his form, he did not win selection for England again until the Indian tour of 1963/64, where at Kanpur he bowled 71 overs for just 67 runs.

Despite being overlooked time and again by the England selectors, Mortimore continued to form a highly effective partnership with David Allen. Their contrasting styles complemented each other well, and whilst Allen was a bigger spinner of the ball, it was Mortimore's guile and exceptional accuracy that helped to snare him so many wickets, as he carefully plotted a batsman's downfall, often through a lengthy series of deliveries.

Mortimore was a classical off-spinner with the ability to sharply spin the ball, besides floating one past the outside edge. In 1964, he took over a hundred wickets again for Gloucestershire, before taking a well-deserved benefit the following year. 1965 proved to be an important year for the off-spinner as he was appointed the

County captain, and he brought to the role the same thoughtful and studious approach that he paid to his bowling. His tenure lasted three years, during which the County remained in the second half of the table, but by the time he handed over the reins, the County were in a healthier state both on and off the field, with new young blood starting to emerge.

It was therefore quite fitting for Mortimore to continue his playing career into the 1970s, and despite spending time on accountancy exams, his accurate off-spin met with success in the new form of limited over cricket. Despite being in the veteran stage, Mortimore's dependable bowling was an integral part of the County's success in the Gillette Cup of 1973, with the wily spinner delivering his 12 overs in the final against Sussex for just 32 runs.

Born: 3 March 1904, Berkeley
Died: 26 October 1955, Gloucester

Batting

M	I	NO	Runs	Av
452	700	79	14751	23.75

50	100	ct/st		
72	14	229		

Bowling

Balls	Runs	Wkts	Av	5wI	10wM
6231	3970	100	39.70	1	-

Best Performances
145* v Hampshire at Southampton, 1927
6-9 v Somerset at Bristol, 1937

Billy Neale was a member of a famous farming dynasty based in the Berkeley Vale, and the gentleman farmer thought nothing of supervising the milking on the family's Breadstone Farm before driving down to the County Ground in Bristol. Hunting was also in his family's blood, whilst several relations excelled at other sports. Billy's uncle Maurice had been a talented rugby three-quarter for Bristol and Blackheath alongside C.B. Fry, besides winning International honours with England.

Billy became a close friend of Wally Hammond, and a contemporary of the great batsman in both the Gloucestershire side, and at school in Cirencester. After some fine innings, both for the grammar school and the Cirencester club, Neale followed Hammond onto the Gloucestershire staff in the early 1920s, and the pair later shared a record fourth-wicket stand of 321 against Leicestershire at Gloucester.

He was one of the few players to form a quite close and lasting friendship with the taciturn Hammond. During the summer holidays from Cirencester Grammar School, Wally would stay with the Neales on their farm. Even in adulthood, he really enjoyed, with more than a touch of envy, the company of the illustrious and well-connected Neales. Billy was still with

the club as an adhesive and dependable middle order batsman when his great pal Hammond finally called it a day before the start of the 1947 season. By the end of 1948, Billy had followed suit and retired from the County game.

In his early years, Billy had played as an amateur, and in 1927 he hit hundreds in consecutive matches, including a career best 145* against Hampshire at Southampton. The fickle economics of agriculture no doubt prompted Billy to turn professional in 1929 and he continued to be a steadying influence in the County's middle order, displaying an uncomplicated technique out in the middle, and a kind-hearted manner off the field.

His most successful season was in 1938, when he aggregated 1,488 runs and hit five assured and attractive centuries. Success never went to Billy's head, and even in his later years he remained a modest fellow, grateful for having the chance to enjoy a good day's sport and to return home at night to his beloved Berkeley Vale. By his own admission, Billy was surrounded by more aggressive and talented stroke-makers in Gloucestershire's batting line-up. But they often only got the chance to flourish because of Billy's watchful defence and steady support at the other end.

In his youth, Billy had been quite a handy leg-spinner, and later in his professional career, Billy developed a reputation of having a golden arm, taking 6 for 9 in 25 balls against Somerset at Bristol in 1937.

Ronald Bernard Nicholls
RHB & OB, 1951-1975

Born: 4 December 1933, Sharpness
Died: 21 July 1994, Montpellier, Cheltenham

Batting

M	I	NO	Runs	Av
534	954	52	23608	26.17
87	84	2	1740	21.22

50	100	ct/st
124	18	286/1
10	1	12

Bowling

Balls	Runs	Wkts	Av	5wI	10wM
1166	719	11	65.36	-	-
6	4	1	4.00		

Best Performances
217 v Oxford University at Oxford, 1962
2-19 v Glamorgan at Neath, 1964
127 v Berkshire at Reading, 1966
1-4 v Berkshire at Reading, 1966

Ron Nicholls is the fourth highest scorer in Gloucestershire's history, with only Hammond, Milton and Dipper having scored more runs for the County. It was a fine reward for a talented all-round sportsman who mixed a successful and loyal career in County cricket with winters playing professional football, keeping goal for Bristol Rovers, Cardiff City, Bristol City and Cheltenham Town.

After completing his National Service, Ron emerged in the late 1950s as a fluent and quite flamboyant stroke-maker, with some of his classy shots drawing favourable comparison to those of Tom Graveney. Ron passed a thousand runs in 1957 and 1958, with the latter season witnessing his maiden century against County Champions Surrey at Bristol. For no less than four and a half hours he defied the illustrious Surrey attack with a display of sound driving, fierce cuts, strong pulls, and deft glances off his legs, and had rain not intervened on the final day, his efforts might even have helped Gloucestershire to victory.

In 1961, Ron moved up the order to open the batting when Martin Young was injured. The greater responsibility this brought helped to curb a certain impetuous streak in his batting, and four centuries, all compiled in a more workmanlike vein, more than justified his elevation up the order and helped him to go from strength to strength in the following seasons. Indeed, 1962 was his most productive season, with Ron amassing 2,059 runs, including a career-best 217 against Oxford University at The Parks and a share in a record opening stand of 395 with Martin Young.

Ron had another good summer in 1964, topping the County's batting averages with over 1,900 runs, and his finest innings came in the local derby with Somerset, where he struck a belligerent 92 to see his team to a five-wicket success on the final afternoon.

As with his promotion up the order, Ron easily adapted to the new demands of one-day cricket and took the changes in his stride, like everything else he did on the cricket field, without the trace of any fuss or flamboyance. His reward came in 1966, as he became the first Gloucestershire batsman to score a century in limited-overs cricket, with 127 in the Gillette Cup tie against Berkshire at Reading.

Although he hailed from Sharpness, Ron's spiritual home was Cheltenham. It was here that he had first played club cricket with Cheltenham Town, and it was where he continued to enjoy coaching and playing after retiring from the County scene in 1974, often proudly appearing alongside his two sons. For a while, Ron also led the Gloucestershire Second XI, and it was typical of the fine team man that he answered an SOS to reappear in 1975 when the County were beset by an injury crisis.

Born: 11 April 1911, Montpellier, Cheltenham
Died: 2 September 1936, Cirencester

Batting

M	I	NO	Runs	Av
106	167	7	2993	18.70
50	100	ct/st		
11	1	76		

Bowling

Balls	Runs	Wkts	Av	5wI	10wM
57	36	0	-	-	-

Best Performances
116 v Kent at Gloucester, 1936

Dallas Page, Gloucestershire's captain in 1935 and 1936, died at the age of twenty-five, after being injured in a car accident. The tragedy occurred after he had led the County to an innings victory over Nottinghamshire in the final match of the 1936 season.

While driving from the Gloucester ground to his home in Cirencester, Page's sports car collided with a motorcyclist and crashed into a Cotswold stone wall. At first, his injuries did not appear to be too severe and after climbing from the wreckage, he was taken to Cirencester Memorial Hospital for a check-up. But it subsequently transpired that he had suffered major internal injuries, and he died early the next morning.

His father, Herbert Page, had played for Gloucestershire from 1883, and had led the County in 1885 and 1886 before taking up a teaching post at Cheltenham College. Dallas inherited his father's love of sport and developed into a fine schoolboy sportsman,

playing with distinction as a fly half, and winning a place in the school's XI in 1928 and 1929. Whilst at Cheltenham, he was also coached by Billy Woof, who had played under Dallas' father in the Gloucestershire side of the 1880s.

After leaving Cheltenham, Dallas attended Sandhurst with thoughts of seeking a commission with the Gloucestershire Regiment. However, his career changed track at the end of the 1934 season as the twenty-three year old accepted the offer to take over from Bev Lyon as Gloucestershire's captain.

Page had made his Gloucestershire debut the previous season, and during both 1933 and 1934 he had played several attractive innings for the County, besides being a fine cover point. He had a modest first season in charge, as Gloucester-shire slipped down to fifteenth place in the Championship, winning just 6 games. But the young captain put these disappointments well behind him in 1936, and guided the County back up to fourth place in the table. He also recorded his maiden Championship century, scoring 116 against Kent at Gloucester, and playing a series of fluent and forcing drives on both sides of the wicket.

By common consent, Page was starting to show great flair as the County's leader, and he had seemed destined for a long and successful County career. Tragically, this was not to be the case.

Arthur James Paish
LHB & SLA, 1898-1903

Born: 5 April 1874, Gloucester
Died: 16 August 1948, Gloucester

Batting

M	I	NO	Runs	Av
79	123	38	967	11.37
50	100	ct/st		
1	-	79		

Bowling

Balls	Runs	Wkts	Av	5wl	10wM
18389	8611	354	24.32	27	7

Best Performances
66 v Kent at Gravesend, 1901
8-68 v Warwickshire at Edgbaston, 1899

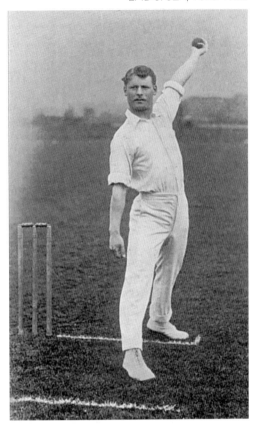

Arthur Paish had a meteoric rise from club cricket in Gloucester into the world of County cricket. In 1899, only his second season with the County, the left-arm spinner took over a hundred wickets, but the short and sturdy Paish had a very peculiar action, and with increasing concerns about the legality of his action, he left the County at the end of the 1903 season.

He had joined the County's staff in 1898 following the desire by Gloucestershire to hire some young rising professionals. But the twenty-three year old only made a single appearance, appropriately enough against Lancashire at the Spa Ground in his native Gloucester. It did not prove to be fairytale start for the young spinner, as the weather prevented a positive outcome, and he remained wicket-less in eleven overs.

Few could have predicted what would happen the following year, as the virtually unknown spinner had a dramatic rise to become, in the words of *Wisden's* correspondent, 'by far and away the best bowler on the side, taking 125 wickets for a little under 19 runs each'. He was equally effective both at home and away, taking nine wickets at The Oval, followed by fourteen in the return contest at Cheltenham. He also claimed ten wickets in the match with Sussex at Brighton, twelve in the contest with Warwickshire at Edgbaston and ten in the game with Essex at Clifton College.

Some of the County's supporters even started to talk about Paish going on to play in Test cricket, but in the next two seasons, he only

took 83 and 94 wickets, and proved to be more expensive than in 1899, losing his accuracy of length and spin. His confidence was also knocked by a few dark mutterings about the legality of his jerky action and, after a poor start to the start of the 1902 season, Paish was dropped from the Gloucestershire team.

He returned to the side in 1903, but the whispers about his action continued, and in the match against Nottinghamshire at Bristol, Paish took 8-90, but was also called for an unfair delivery by umpire Bill West. He also stood in Gloucestershire's next home game against Yorkshire at the County Ground, and on the second morning of the game he called Paish four times for throwing. Despite remedial work in the nets, Paish could not regain his powers of spin with his remodelled action, and at the end of the season, he left the County's staff and returned to club cricket in Gloucester. He later acted as groundsman at the Wagon Works ground.

RHB & SLA, 1903-1935

Born: 14 October 1882, Prestbury
Died: 11 July 1959, Cranleigh, Surrey

Batting

M	I	NO	Runs	Av
602	916	186	7616	10.43
50	100	ct/st		
9	-	236		

Bowling

Balls	Runs	Wkts	Av	5wI	10wM
152097	61600	3169	19.43	272	91

Best Performances

82 v Leicestershire at Leicester, 1921
10-79 v Somerset at Bristol, 1921

Charlie Parker is, and is likely to remain, the most prolific wicket-taker ever to play County cricket for Gloucestershire. In a wonderful career spanning nearly thirty seasons, the left-arm spinner claimed 3,170 victims for his County, and 3,278 in all first-class matches, with only Wilfred Rhodes and 'Tich' Freeman having ever taken more wickets in English cricket. He also dismissed Don Bradman twice in Gloucestershire's match with the Australians in 1930 and so bamboozled the great batsman that he never opted to play against Gloucestershire on subsequent visits.

Parker began his career as an orthodox left-arm seamer before converting to spin in 1919 when George Dennett was still on active service. He still bowled a few overs of seam with the new ball, but his career took a dramatic upswing as a spinner, taking 125 wickets in 1920, and over a hundred for every season until his retirement in 1935. In his benefit match against Yorkshire in 1922, he took 9-36 and achieved the remarkable feat of hitting the stumps with five successive deliveries – one of which was a no-ball. Three years later against Essex at Gloucester, he broke W.G.'s County record for the best ever match analysis for Gloucestershire, with returns of 8-12 and 9-44 as he completely confounded the visiting batsmen.

As one colleague remembered, he was 'lithe and over six feet tall; he would glide through a day's bowling with unbuttoned shirt sleeves flapping about his wrists, always with a cap pulled down at a rakish angle over his right eye, and a smooth effortless rhythm that did not change as the overs passed.

He bowled with the precision of a machine and was rarely collared.' Even on the most docile of wickets, Parker's immaculate length, puzzling flight and sharp spin posed problems for the best of County batsmen. With Wally Hammond taking many fine catches at slip (including a record 8 off Charlie's bowling against Surrey at Cheltenham in 1928), it seemed that every edge or mistake resulted in a wicket for Parker.

His approach to bowling on turning wickets was, in his own words, 'to try to stop batsmen using their feet against you. On a good pitch, however, it's the opposite – keep it in the air as long as possible. In doing so, you'll keep it above the batsman's eye level, and if he can't see above the flight, he'll have great difficulty in judging line and length.'

Despite being a shade quicker than most of his type, Parker had few peers as a left-arm spinner in County cricket, yet he only played once for England – in the Fourth Test of the 1921 Ashes series at Old Trafford. The match was spoilt by rain, but Parker still took 2-32 from 28 overs before returning to Bristol for the local derby with Somerset and taking 10-79 as Gloucestershire won by one wicket. Despite Charlie being in fine form, the selectors looked elsewhere for the remaining games of the series, and over the next few years he was regularly overlooked.

In 1926, he was called into the England squad for the games at Headingley and Old Trafford. Both of the wickets were likely to assist his spin, with the press even calling them 'Parker pitches'. But again, other bowlers got the nod, and after being left out at Manchester in favour of Greville Stevens, the Oxford University leg-break bowler, Parker was more than a bit miffed at being made twelfth man. Indeed, when asked to take drinks out onto the field, he is reputed to have told Arthur Carr, the English captain, 'If you wanted someone to do that, you should have selected a waiter instead!'

Indeed, his omission from the Test side may have stemmed from the fact that to some, Charlie had a reputation of being a difficult man and a person who was not afraid to speak his mind. However, contemporaries at County level offer a different view, remembering that after a furious glare from Parker for dropping a catch, you were just as likely to get a broad grin a few balls later. Quick-tempered he may well have been, but Charlie was certainly not too difficult to handle.

Perhaps it was his radical political ideas that really ruffled a few feathers within the establishment. Charlie had always held a deep interest in politics, and whilst a young boy at Cheltenham Grammar School he had enjoyed reading books on political theory, especially Marxist ideology. By adulthood, he was very much of the opinion that everyone was equal, and he certainly did not subscribe to the belief that he should doff his cap to a person simply because they were of wealthy or noble descent.

Over the years, he crossed swords with several toffs in the higher echelons of the MCC and made no secret of the fact that he would never be chosen for England whilst Sir Pelham Warner was a Test selector. Indeed, after the Gloucestershire dinner of 1929 in Bristol's Grand Hotel, an altercation took place between the two men in the hotel lift. After being asked by the attendant to 'make room for Mr Warner', Charlie apparently grasped Sir Pelham's lapels and delivered such a broadside about Warner being the one person who had blighted his Test career that Sir Pelham turned as white as a sheet.

Given his years of success at County level, his frustration was understandable, but in fact Warner may not have been the guilty party, and the following year he was included by the selectors in the twelve for the Fifth Test at The Oval. However, it proved to be another fruitless journey, and on this occasion it was Bob Wyatt, rather than Sir Pelham, who made the final decision to omit Charlie. However, Wyatt later admitted to regretting his decision, writing in his memoirs that 'maybe it was a mistake to leave Parker out.'

Charlie duly returned to the West Country for Gloucestershire's match against the Australians and immediately proved the folly of his omission from the Test side. As the tourists chased a victory target on the final afternoon, Charlie and his spin partner, Tom Goddard, tricked and teased the Australians. When the match ended in a famous tie, Charlie walked off the pitch with figures of 7-54, and received the congratulations of hundreds of delighted Bristolians.

During the 1930s, Parker formed a most potent partnership with Goddard, with the young off-spinner's emergence easing the workload on the veteran left-armer. It also extended Parker's glittering career, allowing him to claim 100 wickets a year when into his fifties, before retiring in 1935, having taken over 2,800 wickets at around 18 runs apiece following his conversion to spin.

Grahame Wilshaw Parker

RHB & RM, 1932-1950

Born: 11 February 1912, Gloucester
Died: 11 November 1995, Sidmouth, Devon

Batting

M	I	NO	Runs	Av
70	112	9	1954	18.97

50	100	ct/st		
4	4	54		

Bowling

Balls	Runs	Wkts	Av	5wI	10wM
3177	1366	32	42.68	1	-

Best Performances
210 v Kent at Dover, 1937
5-57 v Warwickshire at Edgbaston, 1934

Grahame Parker was Gloucestershire's secretary/manager from 1968 until 1976, and in 1986/87 he served as the County's president. During his time in office, Parker displayed the same genial mix of authority and gentle understanding that had made him a successful schoolmaster – firstly at Dulwich College, and later at Blundell's School, where he ran the geography department and was a house master for fifteen years.

Indeed, Parker was the archetypal school teacher amateur, cramming as many fixtures as possible into his holidays, and playing for the love of the game rather than for financial reward. As well as being a talented cricketer, Parker was also an outstanding rugby player. Whilst at the Crypt School in Gloucester, he represented both the school and the town as an agile and quick-thinking scrum-half.

In 1932, he went up to Selwyn College, Cambridge, where he became a fine full-back and won his rugby blue. His brave tackling and ability to kick off both feet impressed many fine judges, and after some exceptional performances for Blackheath and Gloucestershire, he won selection twice for England in 1938. Parker also marked his debut against Ireland with an immaculate display of kicking, converting six of the seven tries, and scoring a penalty for good measure, as the rampant English team routed their opponents.

On the cricket field, Parker won blues in 1934 and 1935, despite having opted to focus on playing rugby. In fact, he only turned out for the cricket side in 1934 after being persuaded by the captain to help out when a late vacancy arose before the match with Nottinghamshire. Parker went on to score 96 against Larwood and Voce, and subsequently played on a regular basis. Together with the support of Tony Allen, he took part in a record opening partnership of 205 in the 1934 Varsity Match, and the following summer he skilfully led the University to success over Oxford.

After Cambridge, Grahame went into teaching, and in his summer holidays he won a place in the Gloucestershire side as an assertive middle-order batsman and medium-paced swing bowler. He was also a most enthusiastic fielder and still displayed the same eagerness that he had shown on his County debut, where he was thrilled to be taking the field alongside the people he had hero-worshipped as a schoolboy. Even when well into his seventies, there was still a sparkle in Grahame's eyes when he recalled how with a mixture of awe, shock and embarrassment, he had been greeted on his County debut as 'Mr Parker' by his namesake Charlie Parker – his schoolboy hero.

The more dour and muscle-bound professionals must have been pleased at the sight of the young amateur running like a hare in the field and there were times when his youthful exuberance rubbed off on them. Indeed, when Parker made a career best double-century at Dover in 1937, he celebrated his feats in time honoured fashion by buying the team a round of drinks, and even the taciturn Wally Hammond, who rarely socialised with the team, joined him after play.

Michael John Procter
RHB & RFM/OB, 1965-1981

Born: 15 September 1946, Durban

Batting

M	I	NO	Runs	Av
259	437	38	14441	36.19
222	212	14	5579	28.18

50	100	ct/st
70	32	209
31	5	69

Bowling

Balls	Runs	Wkts	Av	5wI	10wM
38276	16299	833	19.56	42	5
9717	5246	279	18.80		

Best Performances
203 v Essex at Gloucester, 1978
8-30 v Worcestershire at Worcester, 1979
154* v Somerset at Taunton, 1972
6-13 v Hampshire at Southampton, 1977

Mike Procter remains amongst the most exciting, inspiring and entertaining of all the overseas players to have graced the County game. He was also a true all-rounder, worth his place either as a batsman or a bowler, and someone, as he proved time and again with Gloucestershire, who could produce a match-winning spell with either bat or ball. In fact, he is the only player to have scored a century and taken a hat-trick on two occasions – for Gloucestershire against Essex in 1972 and Leicestershire in 1979. Through his all-round efforts, 'Proctershire' become one of the most potent one-day teams of the early 1970s, and he subsequently became their inspirational leader.

In essence, Procter was a batsman in the classical mould, readily combining the most elegant of strokes, particularly straight and through the covers, with a wide range of more aggressive and savage blows, especially off the back foot. He loved to score hundreds, and even as a twelve year old at prep school in Natal, Procter scored five centuries, including an unbeaten 210 against a Transvaal side. He never lost this almost insatiable appetite for runs, and in 1970/71, whilst playing for Rhodesia, he scored six centuries in successive innings. The first five came in the Currie Cup, whilst the sixth occurred in an end-of-season friendly against Western Province, when Rhodesia had slumped to 5-3. Procter then turned things around in charac-

teristic fashion, hitting a whirlwind 254 to emulate the feats of two other cricketing greats – C.B. Fry and Sir Don Bradman.

Procter continued in prolific vein when returning to Gloucestershire in 1971, hitting 133 against Leicestershire, before a 79-minute hundred against Middlesex – the fastest of the season – and then another hundred, albeit at a slightly more pedestrian rate of two hours against Somerset at Bristol! However, his fourth and undoubtedly best century of a memorable summer came in the County's four-wicket victory over Yorkshire at Sheffield. Gloucestershire were chasing 201 in 135, but had begun poorly. At tea, and with 85 minutes left, they were 28 for 3. A draw appeared the best they could hope for, but Procter was not one for such defeatist talk, and he proceeded to smash 3 sixes and 17 fours to see his side home with two overs to spare.

Another phenomenal spell of hitting came in 1973, as Procter hit four centuries in eleven days – the first came against Worcestershire at Cheltenham in a match during which he also took three wickets in four balls to see Gloucestershire to a 138-run victory. Warwickshire were the next to suffer, as Procter struck three sixes and 11 fours as the crowd at the Cheltenham Festival applauded another fine century. His third century followed at Worcester, with the fourth coming against a hapless Glamorgan side at Swansea, where Procter picked out, with regular monotony, the short straight boundaries at the St Helen's ground, racing to 152 in 140 minutes with 6 sixes and 17 fours.

As well as these Herculean displays with the bat, Procter was a tearaway and hostile fast bowler, and in the course of his County career he produced some devastating spells. It was a fearsome sight to see him charging in to bowl, with his blond hair bobbing up and down, and delivering the ball chest-on, almost off the wrong foot, with a whirlwind action of his arms. The ball would then speed out, as if being released from a catapult, and often swing in lavishly towards the batsman from a very full length.

One of his most memorable feats of bowling came in Gloucestershire's Benson & Hedges Cup semi-final against Hampshire at Southampton in 1977. In front of the television cameras, he produced a devastating spell, bowling in his opinion as fast as he had ever done in his career. With the fifth ball of his fourth over, he uprooted Gordon Greenidge's stumps, and then with the first three balls of his fifth over he trapped Barry Richards and Trevor Jesty leg before, before bowling John Rice off his pads to claim four wickets in five balls. His opening spell of 6-3-3-4 subsequently became 11-5-13-6 as Gloucestershire won a gripping game and then went on to win the Benson & Hedges Cup itself.

It was as a bowler that he burst onto the Test scene in Australia in 1969/70, with 26 wickets at 13 runs apiece in the four-match series, and when playing for Gloucestershire he was one of the most potent new ball bowlers on the County circuit. In his early years, he bowled from quite wide of the crease, but he subsequently moved closer to the stumps and developed a ball that moved away off the pitch. He still retained his whirlwind action, even though it increasingly placed a great strain on his right knee, and later in his career, he reduced the number of flat-out bursts, opting instead for spells of medium pace. As the true all-rounder, Procter could also sharply spin the ball, and as his career developed, he delivered more and more spells of spin – and with some success, as testified by career best figures of 9-71 for Rhodesia against Transvaal at Bulawayo in 1972/73.

Procter's first appearance in England came in 1963, when he toured the country as vice-captain of the South African schools side. He returned in 1965 with Barry Richards, appearing in club cricket in the Bristol area, in addition to one match for the First XI against the touring Springboks. Their hopes of a place in the Championship side were dashed by the strict regulations on the registration of overseas players, but their revision in 1968 saw Procter return to Gloucestershire on a full-time basis.

It was not long before he had made his mark on the English game, with a hundred against Hampshire and Middlesex – when scoring 134 in a shade over two hours, he completely took apart the bowling of Fred Titmus, one of the most wily off-spinners in the game. Procter then mastered a difficult wicket at Cardiff to score a composed century against Glamorgan, and coupled with some blistering spells of pace bowling, he was in sight of achieving the Double in his first full season with Gloucestershire when he was struck down with a thigh injury.

Over the next thirteen years, Procter proved to be the heartbeat of the County side, and he produced many memorable performances with both bat and ball. His double hundred at Gloucester against Essex in 1978 was described by *Wisden* as 'the best innings seen on the ground since Hammond's heyday'. In 1979, he hit a century and took a hat-trick against Leicestershire at Bristol, before hitting six sixes in successive balls against Somerset, and recording a 57-minute century against Northamptonshire at Bristol.

Charles Thomas Michael Pugh

RHB & OB, 1959-1962

Born: 13 March 1937, Marylebone, London

Batting

M	I	NO	Runs	Av
76	134	8	2324	18.44
50	100	ct/st		
8	1	41		

Bowling

Balls	Runs	Wkts	Av	5wl	10wM
54	30	1	30.00	-	-

Best Performances

137 v Derbyshire at Chesterfield, 1960
1-12 v Kent at Maidstone, 1960

Tom Pugh was the last in a long and illustrious line of amateurs to captain Gloucestershire, and his appointment in 1961 only came after Tom Graveney's departure to Worcestershire.

Pugh had been a fine opening batsman and outstanding racquets player at Eton, and after some success with the MCC and in London club cricket, Pugh's name was given to Sir Percy Lister, Gloucestershire's vice-chairman, by no less a judge than Percy Fender, the former Surrey and England player. Fender believed that Pugh was a man who could prove to be a successful and dynamic leader of a County side, and after watching Pugh bat, Lister invited him to turn out for Gloucestershire in 1959.

Pugh confirmed Percy Fender's judgement by proving himself to be a well-organised batsman, and someone with a fiercely competitive instinct. After rearranging his business commitments, Pugh won a regular place in the County's side in 1960, opened the batting with Martin Young and registered his maiden first-class hundred at Chesterfield with a forthright innings of 137. It came during a record partnership of 256 for the second wicket with Gloucestershire captain Tom Graveney, and their run spree helped to lay the foundations for an innings victory.

This was one of nine Championship successes in what proved to be a quite difficult year both for the club and their captain. It ended with Graveney's departure from the club, and then Pugh's elevation to the County captaincy. If his rise to County captain was a dramatic one, Pugh's first month in charge of the side was

equally eventful. He led the County to victories over Warwickshire and the MCC, but then in mid-May at Peterborough he ducked into a full toss from Northamptonshire's pace bowler David Larter and sustained a broken jaw. Pugh missed the next six weeks, and by the time he had regained fitness, Gloucestershire had slipped down the County table.

They fared much better the following year, with Pugh steering the side to eleven Championship wins, including six in the last eight games. Off the field, he continued to be a very personable young man, and was well liked by the players under his command. Whilst he was a canny tactician, his batting record was very modest and despite his century at Chesterfield, it became clear that the side would be strengthened if another professional batsman was included in his place. Consequently, Pugh stood down at the end of 1962 and returned to the business world, his aspirations as a County batsman largely unfulfilled.

Born: 24 June 1866, Itchington
Died: 9 August 1937, West End, Southampton

Batting

M	I	NO	Runs	Av
91	162	8	2654	17.23
50	**100**	**ct/st**		
10	1	61/4		

Bowling

Balls	Runs	Wkts	Av	5wI	10wM
208	93	3	31.00	-	-

Best Performances
161 v Middlesex at Cheltenham, 1884
1-11 v Surrey at Clifton, 1884

William Pullen was another schoolboy prodigy, making his debut in County cricket at the tender age of 15 years and 2 months. Like many of the other young Gloucestershire amateurs, Pullen was 'discovered' by W.G., although the precociously gifted youngster never reached the dizzy heights in the cricket world that the doctor had predicted.

It was while a schoolboy at Long Ashton School that Pullen had his first taste of County cricket, appearing in the Somerset side for their friendly against Hampshire in 1881. Sensing that the youngster might be snaffled by their neighbours, W.G. was eager to get Pullen involved with Gloucestershire, so the following summer he was invited by the doctor to play for the County's Colts team. A few weeks later, he made his Championship debut for Gloucestershire.

The sixteen year old had an immediate impact, making a cultured 71 against the powerful York-shire side at the Cheltenham Festival. His graceful driving off the front foot, especially through point and the covers, drew rich praise from the apprecia-tive crowd, as well as the many amateurs who felt that Pullen was one of the most talented schoolboys they had ever seen.

But Pullen had other talents and aspirations outside the cricket world, and on leaving school he began training to be an engineer and was attached to the Taff Vale Railway Company, based at Cardiff Docks. Despite his many academic commitments,

Pullen successfully mixed work with pleasure and enjoyed a couple of very profitable summers for Gloucestershire, Cardiff CC and various other wandering sides.

His most prolific season was 1884, when he hit 161 for Gloucestershire against Middlesex at Cheltenham, and a fine 185 when guesting for the South Wales Cricket Club against Kensington Park. However, for the next couple of years, his studies came first, and after playing in a few games in 1885, he did not reappear again on a regular basis until 1887 against Surrey at Moreton-in-Marsh.

Despite an absence from County cricket for over two years, he looked very comfortable at the crease, and in the match against Yorkshire at Dewsbury, Pullen made a bold 78, freely hitting the Yorkshire bowlers whilst several of his team-mates struggled. The following year, he gained a scholarship to study at the Royal School of Mines in South Kensington, but he was still able to be a regular member of the Gloucestershire side in 1888, and on occasions he enthusiastically kept wicket when the County were missing their regular 'keeper. He had a particularly good summer, finishing second to W.G. in the County's batting averages, and he was the star of a fine victory against Sussex at Clifton, making 70 and 45* as Gloucestershire won by 7 wickets.

Despite his success at both club and County level, Pullen steadily devoted more and more of his time to his career as an engineer, and in 1892 he accepted the offer of a post in the Engineering Department at Cardiff University and retired from County cricket.

Octavius Goldney Radcliffe
RHB & OB, 1886-1893

Born: 20 October 1859, North Newnton
Died: 13 April 1940, Cherhill, Calne, Wiltshire

Batting
M	I	NO	Runs	Av
119	219	7	4408	20.79

50	100	ct/st		
19	4	52		

Bowling
Balls	Runs	Wkts	Av	5wI	10wM
5249	2669	98	27.23	2	-

Best Performances
117 v Kent at Bristol, 1892
5-34 v Warwickshire at Bristol, 1889

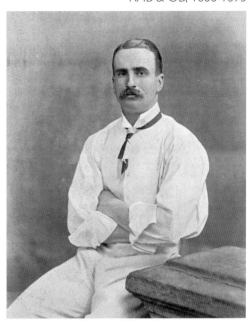

If there were a prize for the most colourful name in Gloucestershire's history, Octavius Goldney Radcliffe would surely be the winner. But there was more to Radcliffe than just the decadent grandeur of his wonderful name, as he was a very reliable and prolific stroke-maker, opening the batting on many occasions with W.G.

Indeed, his successful opening partnership and friendship with the doctor led to Radcliffe being chosen in Lord Sheffield's team that Grace helped to assemble for a tour to Australia in 1891/92. In his famous book, *Cricket*, W.G. described Radcliffe as 'one of the most punishing and dangerous bats in England'. Rich praise indeed, especially for someone who was an entirely self-taught cricketer, with Radcliffe only playing his first serious game of cricket when he was seventeen.

Radcliffe's subsequent progress was both swift and successful, and after some very promising performances with Yatton CC, he won a place in the Somerset side in 1884 and in five appearances, he hit a forceful 101 against Surrey at The Oval. The following year, he transferred his allegiance to Gloucestershire, and began a successful career which saw him remain in the County's side until 1893.

However, his 'transfer' from Somerset was seen in some quarters as a defection, and followed some gentle persuasion from W.G., who was highly impressed with Radcliffe's orthodox style and solid defence, as well as the crispness of his attacking strokes. Whatever the rights or wrongs, it proved to be a most successful switch for Radcliffe, the son of a Wiltshire vicar, who went on to score over 500 runs in 1886 and 1889.

Amongst his finest innings were 104* against Middlesex at Lord's in 1886, 101* against Kent at Canterbury in 1889, and 116 against Lancashire at Old Trafford in 1891. Radcliffe also struck a very forceful 99 against the 1888 Australians at Clifton, showing his class against the tourists before falling one short of a most well deserved century.

Radcliffe twice played for the Gentlemen against the Players, and was a member of Lord Sheffield's team to Australia in 1891/92 – at the time, the party was considered to be the strongest ever to represent England in Australia. Surrounded by so many illustrious names, Radcliffe played mainly in the up-country games, and met with little success but thoroughly enjoyed the experience and the company of such fine cricketers.

After retiring from playing for Gloucestershire in 1894, he moved back to his native Wiltshire and became a dynamic influence in their early years as a Minor County. He led by example with both bat and ball, and against Bedfordshire at Dunstable in 1895 his skilfully flighted off-breaks saw Radcliffe return figures of 5-11.

Born: 1 April 1862, Mickleton
Died: 7 April 1936, Bristol

Batting

M	I	NO	Runs	Av
260	410	151	1922	7.42
50	100	ct/st		
-	-	97		

Bowling

Balls	Runs	Wkts	Av	5wI	10wM
51952	21162	963	21.97	62	8

Best Performances
38 v Yorkshire at Bradford, 1892
8-40 v Kent at Maidstone, 1897

In July 1887, Fred Roberts produced one of the most dramatic ever bowling performances on debut in his first game for Gloucestershire. He took seven wickets in both the first and second innings of the match against Yorkshire at Dewsbury, and subsequently became one of the mainstays of the County's attack for the next sixteen summers.

His eventful introduction to County cricket followed a decision earlier in 1887 by the Gloucestershire committee 'to recruit a resident professional bowler with the least possible delay.' For several weeks, W.G. Grace scouted around local club cricket, and contacted representatives from many leagues, but without success, until he saw the twenty-five-year-old bowler from Mickleton, on the Warwickshire and Worcestershire border.

Impressed by his pace and swing, Grace immediately signed up the left-armer, and his fourteen-wicket haul at Dewsbury confirmed the doctor's assessment of Roberts' abilities. He soon formed a formidable bowling partnership with Billy Woof, and later that year the pair completely overwhelmed the Kent batsmen at Moreton-in-Marsh, bowling out the visitors for just 28, Woof taking 5-18 and Roberts 5-8.

He subsequently proved to be a most valuable acquisition to the club's ranks, with the burly bowler imparting great swing on the ball, and for season after season, his swift in-duckers and fast away swingers deceived many of the country's finest batsmen.

Roberts thrived on hard work and, as was quite common in those days, he frequently bowled unchanged throughout an innings. In the match against Surrey at Bristol in 1903, he and slow left-armer Dennett bowled throughout both of visitors' innings. Their efforts were not in vain, as Gloucestershire won by 18 runs, with Roberts taking 11-93 from his 40 overs. It was a highly impressive performance for a forty-one year old, especially as in the previous ten days he had bowled 85 overs at the Cheltenham Festival to take 9-82 against Kent and 13-94 against Worcestershire.

But the big-hearted and genial bowler was a glutton for hard work, and in 1901 he claimed a career best 119 wickets – despite it being a thoroughly modest season for Gloucestershire, who finished up just one place from the bottom of the County table.

Roberts was a quite modest tail-end batsman, but in 1903 against Sussex at Bristol, Roberts shared in a tenth-wicket stand of 104 with W.S.A. Brown. He reappeared in one match in 1905 when the County were short, before joining the umpire's list and standing in first-class matches from 1906 until 1919.

Douglas Charles Robinson

RHB & WK, 1905-1926

Born: 20 April 1884, Lawrence Weston, Bristol
Died: 29 July 1963, Charlton Kings, Cheltenham

Batting

M	I	NO	Runs	Av
124	216	12	3584	17.56
50	100	ct/st		
14	1	78/26		

Best Performance

150* v Worcestershire at Worcester, 1912

Lieutenant-Colonel Douglas Robinson was a member of the family that owned the famous Bristol paper manufacturing company. Besides playing with distinction for Gloucestershire, and acting as their captain during the mid-1920s, Robinson combined a successful life in business with a distinguished military career that saw him win the Military Cross for gallantry during the First World War.

He might also have won an England cricket cap, as some fine performances with the bat for both Gloucestershire and the Army had resulted in the sturdy wicketkeeper batsman winning a place on the MCC tour to South Africa in 1913/14. After securing leave of absence from the Army, he travelled to the Cape as understudy to Herbert Strudwick. However, as soon as the party arrived in South Africa, Robinson was struck down with illness and was ruled out of the entire tour.

Robinson had been a hard-hitting right-handed batsman and a competent wicketkeeper, who initially won a place in the Marlborough XI, before making his County debut in 1905. The following year he gained a commission in the King's Own Royal Lancaster Regiment, and when his battalion were posted to Colchester, he appeared in seven matches for Essex in 1908. Soon afterwards, they returned to the West Country and Robinson regained his place in the Gloucestershire side.

His military duties prevented him from playing for Gloucestershire on a regular basis, but even so, he produced some impressive displays of powerful hitting, and in 1912 he struck a career best 150* against Worcestershire at New Road. Despite being heavily built, he was an agile wicketkeeper, and was chosen on several occasions to play for the Gentlemen against the Players between 1912 and 1919. In the latter year, he was also a member

of the Gentlemen's team that defeated the Australian Imperial Forces at Lord's by an innings and 133 runs.

He played little County cricket in the early 1920s, but after retiring from the Army in 1924, Robinson took over the captaincy of Gloucestershire. It proved to be a damp summer, and a quite difficult one for the County club, but Robinson, drawing heavily on his military experience, proved to be a tactful and diplomatic captain, cheerfully cajoling the assorted mix of hard-nosed professionals and cavalier amateurs at his disposal. Despite not having a vast pool of talent available, Robinson's efforts resulted in Gloucestershire rising up the table into sixth place, after winning 10 of their 28 matches.

This was, though, his most successful season in charge, as the following year the side slipped back to tenth place, and then fifteenth in 1926, after which Robinson stood down from the captaincy. Although he spent the next few years in the business world of Bristol, he still found time to play for the MCC, as well as I Zingari and other wandering elevens. His final appearance in representative cricket came on the tour by Lionel Tennyson's XI to Jamaica in 1927/28, where he and the Glamorgan wicketkeeper Dennis Sullivan shared duties behind the stumps during the five-week tour.

Sir Foster Gotch Robinson

RHB & WK, 1903-1923

Born: 19 September 1880, Sneyd Park, Bristol
Died: 31 October 1967, East Harptree, Somerset

Batting

M	I	NO	Runs	Av
68	116	2	2075	18.20
50	100	ct/st		
8	2	46/28		

Best Performance
144 v Essex at Colchester, 1920

match in May 1900, he failed to win a blue. In 1903, he made his County debut and, like so many of the other young amateurs, he only appeared occasionally for the County side during the next decade as the demands of the business world took precedence. Even so, he was able to regularly turn out for the Clifton club, and in 1912 he was appointed as their captain.

Robinson proved to be an astute and capable leader, and when Gloucestershire re-grouped after the First World War, he was invited to act as their captain in 1919, while the County resumed their activities with a series of two-day matches. He proved his leadership abilities by leading the County to four victories, but met with little personal success with the bat.

However, he retained the captaincy for 1920 and he celebrated the resumption of Championship cricket with centuries against Essex and Worcestershire. During the summer, Robinson also received a letter from the headmaster of Cirencester Grammar School outlining the feats of a young batsman called Walter Hammond, who had made 365* in a house match. Foster invited the schoolboy for a trial during the cricket week at Clifton, and he was duly impressed with Hammond's abilities.

'He'll become a second Jack Hobbs,' Robinson remarked to club officials as they watched the youngster bat with aplomb, and his performance was sufficient for Robinson to invite Hammond to play for the County during the Cheltenham Festival. The rest, as far as Hammond was concerned, was history, as the Cirencester schoolboy went on to become one of the greatest batsmen ever to play for the County. How different it might all have been if Robinson had not acted on that letter.

Sir Foster Robinson was a very colourful, but talented amateur batsman, who was also a leading light in the commercial world of Bristol. He also led the County after the First World War and was responsible for introducing Wally Hammond into County cricket – for that alone Gloucestershire's supporters could be eternally grateful to the influential businessman.

Besides cricket, Foster Robinson had a number of sporting interests, including golf, fishing and horse-racing – he was a noted owner and breeder of thoroughbreds, in addition to being a member of the Jockey Club. Like his cousin Douglas, he was also an active member of the family's highly successful paper manufacturing company in Bristol. Foster served as chairman of the company from 1929 until 1961, as well as holding similar positions with Bristol Waterworks between 1935 and 1960. Indeed, it was his sterling efforts in the business world that saw him receiving a knighthood in 1936.

Robinson had been a fine schoolboy wicketkeeper and a sound middle-order batsman in the Clifton XI between 1895 and 1899. He subsequently went up to Exeter College, Oxford where, despite an appearance in the Freshman's

Peter Rochford
RHB & WK, 1952-1957

Born: 27 August 1928, Halifax, Yorkshire
Died: 18 June 1992, Stroud

Batting

M	I	NO	Runs	Av
80	113	22	479	5.26
50	100	ct/st		
-	-	119/33		

Bowling

Balls	Runs	Wkts	Av	5wI	10wM
-	-	-	-	-	-

Best Performance
31* v Oxford University at The Parks, 1956

Peter Rochford had an all-too-brief County career in the 1950s, yet in the opinion of many who saw the Yorkshireman behind the stumps, he was one of the finest wicketkeepers ever to appear for Gloucestershire.

Peter had shown rich promise as a schoolboy, playing for Scarborough and Yorkshire Second XI, before moving to the West Country and joining the Gloucestershire staff in 1952, as understudy to Andy Wilson. He duly made the position his own in 1954, with his deft and unobtrusive glove-work more than compensating for his limited ability as a batsman.

With razor-sharp reflexes and soft hands, Peter made wicket-keeping look the easiest job in the world. He also developed an almost innate understanding with Bomber Wells – who was not the easiest spinner to read – and after a series of impressive performances behind the stumps, Peter was even talked about as a reserve wicketkeeper for an MCC tour.

Sadly, this particular gem was not without its flaws, and within two years, Peter had left the County's staff. Despite his neat, lounge-suited appearance, Peter was not someone who readily conformed, and he hated too many restrictions. When on form, the club officials turned a blind eye to his indiscretions and excesses off the field, but it was a completely different matter when he lost form in 1957. After one brush too many with the authorities, he left the staff.

Some hoped that Peter would sort himself out and eventually return to County cricket, but this was not to be in a playing capacity. He became an advanced coach, and held coaching positions in various schools, before becoming a first-class umpire and standing in Championship cricket between 1975 and 1977.

Peter subsequently moved to Stroud, where he watched and admired the talents of the young Jack Russell. He would frequently pass on tips and encouragement to the Stroud schoolboy, and it brought a smile to Peter's face to see the youngster go on to join the County's staff and eventually play for England.

In the minds of many long-standing observers of Gloucestershire cricket, only Russell has surpassed Rochford's superiority as a wicketkeeper since the Second World War. He subsequently became a cricket writer and was a journalist with several national newspapers. He had also started work on a book on Denis Compton when he was told the tragic news that he was suffering from throat cancer. In June 1992, Peter collapsed and died in the arms of a fellow customer in one of the quiet little pubs in Stroud where he regularly reminisced about cricket, and tried to forget about his awful illness.

As David Foot later wrote, 'cricket was Peter's life and consuming interest. He never fell out of love with the game, only with fate itself.'

Paul William Romaines ————————————
RHB & RM, 1982-1991

Born: 25 December 1955, Bishop Auckland

Batting

M	I	NO	Runs	Av
161	288	21	7602	28.47
148	136	15	3517	29.07

50	100	ct/st		
38	12	66		
20	2	35		

Bowling

Balls	Runs	Wkts	Av	5wI	10wM
257	247	4	61.75	-	-

Best Performances

186 v Warwickshire at Nuneaton, 1982
3-42 v Surrey at The Oval, 1985
125 v Nottinghamshire at Bristol, 1985

It was definitely a case of second time lucky for Paul Romaines, born and bred in County Durham, who had initially followed the example of other young cricketers from the north-east and had joined the staff at Northamptonshire in 1973. He also reached a final trial for English Schools. However, things did not turn out well with Northants, and in 1976 he left their staff and returned to League cricket.

However, he still had the burning ambition to make the grade as a first-class cricketer, and in 1980 he sent letters to every County, asking for a trial. Only four Counties replied, including Gloucestershire, who duly gave Romaines a new lease of life by inviting the right-handed opening batsman to Bristol in May 1981. At first, it looked like nothing would come of it, as rain washed out several games, but Romaines' luck changed with a century against Somerset's Second XI, and he secured a contract for the following year.

After his disappointments with Northants, he was determined not to let this second chance slip away and over the next ten years he became one of Gloucestershire's most reliable top-order batsmen. An injury to Chris Broad saw Romaines make his Gloucestershire debut in June 1982, and when the England opener regained fitness, Romaines dropped down to the number three spot. But at the end of July it looked like Romaines might lose his place in the side, and before the match with Warwickshire at Nuneaton, captain David Graveney told the Geordie that he would be dropped if he failed again.

Romaines responded with a match-saving innings of 186 batting for almost five hours and hitting 25 fours and 3 sixes.

After a winter of grade cricket in Sydney, Romaines returned to the UK as a less cautious and more complete stroke-player, especially off the front foot. He duly enjoyed a productive season in 1983, with 1,233 runs in Championship cricket, including hundreds against Kent, Worcestershire and Yorkshire, and he deservedly won his County cap.

He went from strength to strength in 1984, passing the 1,800-run mark, with four further Championship centuries, and had his form not tailed off in the final weeks, he might even have passed 2,000. A spell with Griqualand West and Natal helped him to develop both his batting technique as well as his coaching skills. In 1985, he recorded two centuries in one-day games, with 105 in the Sunday League encounter with Northants, and 125 in the Benson & Hedges cup tie with Nottinghamshire.

For the rest of the 1980s, Romaines continued to be an unruffled and steady opening batsman – one of the many unsung heroes who day in, day out perform in County cricket in front of a few hundred spectators. In 1991, he retired from the first-class game, and became Durham's commercial manager before returning to become Gloucestershire's assistant coach. He later became the cricket coach at Clifton College in 1997.

William Henry Rowlands
RHB, 1901-1928

Born: 30 July 1883, Bristol
Died: 29 June 1948, Kingsdown, Bristol

Batting

M	I	NO	Runs	Av
138	207	14	3248	16.82

50	100	ct/st		
14	2	101		

Bowling

Balls	Runs	Wkts	Av	5wI	10wM
458	281	10	28.10	-	-

Best Performances
113 v Lancashire at Liverpool, 1921
1-0 v Derbyshire at Bristol, 1921

Harry Rowlands was one of many talented amateurs to play sporadically for Gloucestershire on either side of the First World War. Most had left the scene by the 1920s, and the loyalty of the right-handed batsman from Cheltenham was rewarded with the post of County captain in 1927 and 1928.

Rowlands also holds a rather bizarre batting record, having made two centuries for the County, some nineteen years apart. The first came in July 1902, his second summer of County cricket, when he hit an impressive 104 against Somerset at Bath, hitting powerfully all around the wicket to reach a maiden hundred in a shade over two hours. Remarkably, Rowlands' next century for the County did not come until July 1921, when he hit an accomplished 113 in two and three-quarter hours against Lancashire at Liverpool.

At the end of 1921, he told the club's officials that he would only turn out in an emergency – and to all intents and purposes, he retired from the County game.

Nevertheless, he agreed to remain as the club's deputy captain under Sir Philip Williams, and later Douglas Robinson. True to his word, Rowlands helped out the County when they were short, and then at the end of 1926, he stepped into the breach left by Robinson's retirement, leading the County in 1927.

Rowlands duly confirmed the wisdom of his appointment by steering the side up to twelfth place in the table. He commanded great respect for his wide knowledge of the game, friendly manner and infectious enthusiasm, which all helped to bring out the best from the players under him. It may have been no coincidence either that Wally Hammond had his first truly great season with the bat under Rowlands' captaincy, ending 1927 just 31 runs short of 3,000 runs, with an average of 69 and twelve centuries to his name.

The following year, Hammond made 2,825 runs in all matches, took 84 wickets and held 78 catches, and under Rowlands' astute guidance, Gloucestershire rose up to fifth place in the table, winning nine of their 28 Championship fixtures. The forty-five-year-old Rowlands was delighted by the progress the players had made over the previous couple of years, both collectively and individually, but the Quaker knew by August 1928 that the time was right for him to bow out from the County game. He duly handed over the reins of the club in 1929 to Bev Lyon, knowing that he had successfully filled a void and had helped to groom a number of rising stars.

Robert Charles Russell ———————————
LHB & WK, 1981-present

Born: 15 August 1963, Stroud

Batting

M	I	NO	Runs	Av
345	509	106	12420	30.82
382	298	77	5579	25.24
50	**100**	**ct/st**		
68	5	877/98		
23	2	357/77		

Bowling

Balls	Runs	Wkts	Av	5wI	10wM
50	63	1	63.00	-	-

Best Performances
124 v Nottinghamshire at Trent Bridge, 1996
1-4 v West Indians at Bristol, 1991
119* v British Universities at Bristol, 1998

Gloucestershire have been fortunate to be served by a long line of top-class wicketkeepers. In Jack Russell, they have had not only the services of the finest 'keeper in England, but in the eyes of many, the best wicketkeeper in the world.

Spotted by Gloucestershire coach Graham Wiltshire at the age of nine, Russell made his County debut at the age of seventeen against the Sri Lankans, and became the youngest ever player to keep wicket for the side. The schoolboy gave a beautifully neat display of 'keeping, and celebrated his selection by collecting eight victims, with seven catches and a stumping – a record for a debutant and the first of many outstanding displays behind the stumps.

After completing his schooling, Russell replaced his coach and early mentor Andy Brassington in the Gloucestershire side and from 1983 he has subsequently been an ever-present in the Gloucestershire side. In 1995, he acted as the County's captain, and in 1999 he became only the seventh wicketkeeper in the history of the game to take a thousand catches in first-class cricket.

After barely a dozen or so games with the County, many players and umpires regarded Jack as the best young 'keeper in the country, and in 1987 he toured Pakistan as Bruce French's understudy in the England side. When French was injured the following summer, most people expected Jack to be called up to play against the West Indians, but the selectors made a quirky decision by choosing instead Paul Downton and then Jack Richards.

Russell was eventually chosen in 1988 to make his Test debut against the Sri Lankans at Lord's, and he celebrated by making 94 – the highest individual score of the match and, at the time, a career-best score. Jack subsequently became England's first choice behind the stumps – a long overdue decision in the minds of West County supporters – and in the 1989 Ashes series he made a gritty 64 at Lord's, followed by his maiden first-class century in the Old Trafford Test, as Jack defied the Australian bowlers for over six hours. He finished the series against Australia with 21 victims and 314 runs to his name, and was rewarded with selection as one of *Wisden's* Five Cricketers of the Year.

On the 1989/90 tour to the West Indies, Jack played another stubborn innings at Barbados, and his doughty 55, spanning five hours of spirited defence, nearly saved the Fourth Test. After twenty consecutive Tests, he was controversially replaced behind the stumps by Alec Stewart, with the England selectors opting for the Surrey man's superior batting, rather than Jack's craft and class behind the stumps.

Jack's omission was criticised by many, including former England 'keeper Godfrey Evans, who said 'he was discarded not because of anything he'd done wrong, but because Alec was

a better bat and the selectors were trying to cover up for the lack of a proper all-rounder. There was a terrible irony about this – we were the worst Test side in the world, yet our one player of undeniable world-class could not get into the side.'

As Stewart lost form, trying to combine the roles of a top-order batsman and England's wicketkeeper, Jack was restored for the West Indies tour of 1993/94. It was not the happiest of tours for either Jack or the England side, which was battered by the West Indian pace attack, and Jack briefly lost his place in the England team before returning in 1995 for the series with Pakistan, and then the winter tour to South Africa. It proved to be a fine series for the Gloucestershire 'keeper, as in the Second Test at Johannesburg he took 11 catches and broke Bob Taylor's record for the most dismissals in a match for England.

After such immaculate displays behind the stumps and pugnacious little cameos with the bat, Jack remained in the Test side for the home series with India and Pakistan, and then the 1997/98 winter tour to the Caribbean. But he was then omitted for the home series in 1998, and was omitted from the England party for the Ashes tour the following winter. After playing in the Wills One-Day series in October 1998, Jack announced his retirement from international cricket with 54 Test caps and 40 one-day appearances to his name.

Behind his dark sunglasses, and beneath his battered, floppy white sun hat, lies a very patriotic Englishman, and someone with many idiosyncrasies. These have included intensive training routines and pre-ordained diets with vast numbers of cups of tea before play, or eating Weetabix soaked in milk for precisely twelve minutes. Whilst batting against quick bowlers, Jack has also wandered to the side of the crease in between deliveries, to make fidgety little skips and jumps as the pacemen trudge back to their bowling marks.

Short, alert and quick-moving, Jack has been a fine model for aspiring 'keepers, being beautifully balanced behind the stumps, deftly letting the ball come into his soft hands, and rarely having an off day. One of the features of Gloucestershire's recent success in one-day cricket has been Jack's neat and quicksilver displays of keeping, especially standing up to the medium pace bowlers such as Ian Harvey.

He gave a masterclass on the art of wicket-keeping in the 1999 Benson & Hedges Cup final and deservedly won the Man of the Match Award. Indeed, he is in a class of his own whilst standing up to the County's seamers or spinners, and nonchalantly makes outstanding leg-side stumpings look to be almost routine. As well as being an artist behind the stumps, he has excelled with pencil and paint brushes in hand, and what began as a few sketches to wile away time on tour and in rain breaks has developed into a lucrative career, with Russell opening a gallery in Chipping Sodbury.

LHB & LB, 1972-1982

Born: 5 May 1945, Junagadh, Gujarat, India

Batting

M	I	NO	Runs	Av
193	346	19	12012	36.73
167	*163*	*7*	*4978*	*31.91*

50	100	ct/st		
58	25	177		
27	*6*	*39*		

Bowling

Balls	Runs	Wkts	Av	5wI	10wM
8063	4666	138	33.81	I	-
957	*804*	*33*	*24.36*		

Best Performances
203 v Sri Lankans at Bristol, 1981
5-37 v Kent at Bristol, 1973
131 v Somerset at Bristol (Imperial), 1975
3-19 v Oxfordshire at Bristol, 1975

Sadiq is the youngest member of the illustrious Mohammad family whose contribution to Pakistani cricket has been immense. He first played as a schoolboy in domestic cricket in 1959/60 at the age of 14 years and 9 months, before following his older brothers into Test cricket in 1969/70. Sadiq subsequently followed Mushtaq into English County cricket in the early 1970s, and he gave over ten years of loyal service to Gloucestershire as a fluent and brave opening batsman.

The left-hander initially had trials with Northamptonshire and Essex, for whom he played against Jamaica in 1970, in addition to spells as a professional with Nelson in the Lancashire League, and for Poloc in Scotland. In 1972, Sadiq joined Gloucestershire, along with fellow Pakistani Zaheer Abbas, and quickly established himself as a consistent opening batsman. On seven occasions he passed a thousand runs, and in 1976 he scored four centuries in successive innings, including 163* and 150 against Derbyshire at Bristol. He was also a very useful leg-spinner, claiming 5-37 against Kent at Bristol in 1973.

The small and stocky Pakistani was a compact opener, unfurling an array of aggressive cuts and pulls against the fast bowlers, as well as clever and wristy dabs against the spinners. He was also a shrewd little fellow too. He had a habit of introducing himself formally to any new fast bowler in the opposing team, believing that by shaking hands and wishing the newcomer good luck in English cricket, it would decrease the chances of subsequently getting hit by a short bouncer from his new 'friend'.

His plan worked many times until April 1980, when Gloucestershire travelled to Worcestershire and Sadiq came up against Hartley Alleyne, the opponents' new fast bowler from the Caribbean. Before Sadiq had the chance of going through his party piece, the West Indian walked over to where the Gloucestershire batsmen were practising and said to Sadiq and Zaheer, 'You won't remember me, but I bowled against you both in the nets before a Test back home in Barbados.' Having struck the first blow, Alleyne then followed up an hour or so later as Sadiq flashed at a short rising ball, only to be caught behind and become Alleyne's first Championship victim.

Sadiq won 41 Test caps for Pakistan and appeared in the 1975 and 1979 World Cups. He was also a member of Pakistan's touring party to England in 1974 and 1978, to Australia and New Zealand in 1972/73, and to Australia and the West Indies in 1976/77. He took a benefit in 1982, and subsequently played for Cornwall in 1984, in addition to acting as player/coach to Tasmania. His son, Imraan, also played for Gloucestershire in 2000 after winning blues at Cambridge in 1998 and 1999.

Colin James Scott
RHB & RFM/OB, 1938-1954

Born: 1 May 1919, Syston Common
Died: 22 November 1992, Kettering

Batting
M	I	NO	Runs	Av
235	326	43	3376	11.92
50	100	ct/st		
9	-	194		

Bowling
Balls	Runs	Wkts	Av	5wI	10wM
35358	16766	531	31.57	22	2

Best Performances
90 v Surrey at The Oval, 1947
8-90 v Surrey at The Oval, 1953

Colin Scott burst onto the County scene in 1938, with the tall fast bowler forming a potent new-ball partnership with George Lambert. The youngster soon deceived many experienced players with his pace and natural out-swing, and had he not lost six of the next seven seasons to the war, the blond tearaway might have progressed into the England side.

It was a credit to the raw novice that he so quickly adjusted from the friendly world of club cricket with Downend to the cut and thrust of the professional game. And all this with Wally Hammond standing at first slip, and glaring like a fierce sergeant-major, ready to crack the whip and issue a stern rebuke at the earliest opportunity. Fortunately, Lambert lent a reassuring shoulder to the youngster, as well as many wise words, and a close friendship was soon forged, both on and off the field, between the two fast bowlers.

Scott had many assets, not least of which was being double-jointed, and this allowed him to add several variations to his repertoire, each delivered with a wristy flick at the end of his smooth action. Many top order batsmen tied down by Lambert's accuracy must have hoped there would be rich pickings from Scott. But they found Scott's pace and swing to be a real handful and in his second season he took 121 wickets at 22 apiece.

His natural athleticism in the field also allowed him to take many fine catches in the deep, as well as return arrow-like throws that sped straight into the gloves of Andy Wilson. By the second half of 1939, Scott's name was being touted as a budding Test cricketer, but the outbreak of war put paid to any thoughts Scott and his many admirers 'down West' may have harboured that one day he might be playing in Test cricket. Instead, the next six summers saw Scott represent his country in a more deadly environment, and the best years of his cricketing career were lost forever.

In May 1946, as Gloucestershire returned to action in the Championship, all eyes were on Scott and Lambert, as the County's supporters looked forward to a resumption of their lively partnership. But as the season progressed, it became apparent that although he still was full of boyish enthusiasm, Scott had lost much of his zip. In all, he took just 44 wickets in 1946 and 1947, as it became clear that the post-war Scott was a very different animal to the one who, just seven years earlier, had made batsmen hurry and grope in expectation of making firm contact.

He was still a fine fielder, and showed panache at slip as well as in the deep, besides playing several cameos with the bat, including a career-best 90 at The Oval in 1947. But it was bowling that Scott enjoyed above all else, and he practised assiduously in the nets, hoping to recapture his raw pace and nip off the wicket. When these elements of his bowling did not reappear, Scott concentrated on medium-pace seam, but in 1948 and 1949 he only took 51 wickets. He also had a brief flirtation with off-spin, before returning to seam and taking 101 wickets in 1952. After retiring in 1954, he returned to club cricket with Downend, and continued to bowl off-cutters with great success.

Cyril Otto Hudson Sewell

RHB, 1895-1919

Born: 19 December 1874, Pietermaritzburg, South Africa
Died: 19 August 1951, Bexhill-on-Sea, Sussex

Batting

M	I	NO	Runs	Av
158	278	12	6850	25.75
50	**100**	**ct/st**		
32	8	110		

Bowling

Balls	Runs	Wkts	Av	5wI	10wM
398	304	5	60.80	-	-

Best Performances
165 v Surrey at The Oval, 1914
2-35 v Kent at Cheltenham, 1910

Cyril Sewell was Gloucestershire's captain and secretary in the years immediately before the First World War. His father hailed from Cirencester and had been one of the founding members of the Gloucestershire club, before emigrating to South Africa. When Cyril moved to the UK in 1895 to train as a solicitor, he lodged with relatives in the Cotswolds and agreed to play for his father's old county.

The previous summer, the nineteen year old had toured England with the South African side, and despite his inexperience in representative cricket, the youngster was the leading run scorer on the 1894 tour. He duly made his Gloucestershire debut the following year and in August he hit an attractive maiden half-century in the County's brilliant victory at Cheltenham against the powerful Yorkshire side.

Over the next few years, Sewell developed into a fine fielder in the covers. W.G. was so delighted to have the athletic youngster patrolling the covers alongside Gilbert Jessop that he would announce to opponents 'Don't even think about running to my young whippets – they're the best in the country!'

In 1898, Sewell was a member of the Gloucestershire side that rattled up the small matter of 634 against Nottinghamshire at Bristol – a new County record, with Sewell's 108 coming up in just two hours. He continued to help the County during the 1900s, and in 1905 made elegant centuries against Lancashire and Sussex, followed in 1906 by a splendid 107 against Worcestershire during the Chelten-ham Festival. However, his work as a solicitor rarely allowed him to play in the away games.

Nevertheless, he took over the captaincy in 1913, and led the side to victory in eight County games, and guided them up to ninth place in the Championship. But Gloucestershire struggled in 1914, winning just one match, and playing their home matches in front of disappointing crowds. However, Sewell led by example, and enjoyed his most successful season in County cricket, scoring 1,142 runs to put to one side the disappointments of seventeen defeats, to say nothing of far more weightier matters following the news that war had been declared on 4 August. Indeed, he brightened the gloom in the County's final game of the season against Surrey at The Oval, hitting a sparkling 165 scored out of 230 in the space of just two hours.

During the First World War, Sewell served with the 5th Gloucesters, before becoming a major in the Oxfordshire and Buckinghamshire Regiment. He was on active service in Italy until the middle of the 1919 season, and on his return home the veteran readily agreed to turn out for the club as they played a series of two-day friendlies. He soon found his touch again, and was still good enough to score 102 against Kent at Gloucester.

David Robert Shepherd
RHB, 1965-1979

Born: 27 December 1940, Bideford, Devon

Batting

M	I	NO	Runs	Av
282	476	40	10672	24.47
182	172	17	3311	21.36

50	100	ct/st
55	12	95
13	1	34

Bowling

Balls	Runs	Wkts	Av	5wl	10wM
196	106	2	53.00	-	-
8	10	-	-		

Best Performances

153 v Middlesex at Bristol, 1968
1-1 v Northamptonshire at Gloucester, 1968
100 v Glamorgan at Cardiff, 1978

The ruddy face and portly figure of David Shepherd has become a familiar sight on Test grounds all over the world, as the former Gloucestershire batsman has established himself as one of the most respected and popular umpires in international cricket. Despite travelling all over the world, he has remained fiercely loyal to his West Country roots, living in North Devon, where his family's post office in the quiet village of Instow must seem a haven of peace and tranquility away from the hustle and bustle of Test cricket.

During his playing career, he notched up over 10,000 runs, but as colleague David Green observed, 'there was much more to 'Shep' than figures and performances. The club was never quite the same place without his kindness, his humour and his remarkable evenness of temperament; whether things were going well or badly for him personally, all he ever cared about was his team's success.'

1973 saw 'Shep' play perhaps his most important innings for Gloucestershire, during their second round Gillette Cup tie against Surrey at Bristol. His side had slumped to 24 for 5, and it seemed as if they would be making a swift exit from the competition. On arriving at the crease, 'Shep' said to Tony Brown 'we're in a bit of a mess – what's the plan skipper?' – to which Brown replied 'You're to stay here for the rest of the innings 'Shep'.'

He faithfully and courageously carried out his orders, solidly defying the visiting attack, and with sterling support from young David Graveney, he launched a counter-attack that saw his side to a more respectable 169-7, with Shepherd unbeaten on 72. His yeoman efforts galvanised his side's spirits and with Procter bowling with real venom, supported by some live-wire fielding, Gloucestershire won a remarkable game by 19 runs, and went on to win the competition – their first major title since 1877.

In 1977 he was a member of the County's side that won the Benson & Hedges Cup, and they might not have made the final had it not been for an invaluable 60* in the semi-final against Middlesex. The following year, he enjoyed a joint benefit with fellow Devonian Jack Davey, and celebrated this with a century in the Sunday League encounter against Glamorgan at Cardiff, belying his sturdy frame with a host of quick singles. He retired in 1979 and two years later joined the first-class umpires list, where his good humour and cheery manner soon made him a popular figure. He officiated in the 1983 World Cup, and in 1985 stood in his first Test.

By 2001, he had umpired over a hundred One-Day Internationals and more than fifty Tests. He also stood in the finals of the 1996 and 1999 World Cups, and is one of the most respected umpires in world cricket. This reputation has been built on his unstinting fairness, superb judgement, good humour and a wonderful ability to defuse difficult situations with a cheery smile supported by a firm word.

Born: 24 December 1900, Stevenage, Herts.
Died: 17 March 1988, Ham Green, Bristol

Batting

M	I	NO	Runs	Av
423	684	83	15562	25.89
50	100	ct/st		
62	16	173		

Bowling

Balls	Runs	Wkts	Av	5wI	10wM
73806	28394	1165	24.37	66	9

Best Performances

209* v Glamorgan at Cardiff Arms Park, 1935
9-111 v Middlesex at Lord's, 1936

Reg Sinfield, Gloucestershire's cheerful and warm-hearted all-rounder of the inter-war era, played only once for England, in the opening match of the 1938 Ashes series, but to the delight of his many supporters, his first Test victim was Don Bradman.

Sinfield was a highly accurate off-spinner, who always wore his cap, perched at a jaunty angle, when bowling – a characteristic gleefully mimicked by a generation or more of schoolboys as they played their own little games. On four occasions he took over a hundred wickets in a season, and he wholeheartedly assumed the mantle of the club's leading spinner as the career of his good friend Charlie Parker drew to a close in the late 1930s.

Sinfield's slow-medium off-spin looked innocuous, but he had superb control and subtle changes of flight, angle and pace, including a clever arm ball and one that dipped or floated in the air. He used all of these variations year after year to snare and snaffle the finest batsmen in the County game, often with the help of Wally Hammond at slip, holding onto a thin edge from a batsman bemused by Sinfield's clever bowling.

Although he bagged a pair on his Championship debut in 1925, Sinfield also became a very determined opening batsman,

firstly with Alf Dipper and later Charles Barnett. His consistency was reflected in the fact that he exceeded a thousand runs in a season on ten occasions. His steadiness proved the perfect foil for the more aggressive batsmen, in particular Wally Hammond, another of Reg's close friends, and his unflappable outlook allowed Sinfield to be the sheet anchor of many substantial Gloucestershire totals.

On five occasions, Sinfield carried his bat throughout an innings, and in 1935 he compiled a career best 209* against Glamorgan at the Arms Park, showing sound footwork against the Welsh bowlers and a penchant for working the ball through the onside. It was an innings that lasted seven and three-quarter hours, testifying to Sinfield's immense powers of concentration. He then emerged, as fresh as a daisy, from the Cardiff pavilion to take nine wickets as Gloucestershire recorded a comfortable victory.

Sinfield's father was a builder, but young Reg opted not to follow in his footsteps. On leaving school, he joined C.B. Fry's Mercury Nautical Training Ship for Boys, and then the signals staff of the Royal Navy battleship *King George V*. It was on board the training ship, and in spartan conditions that bordered at times on the sadistic, that Sinfield learnt to box, came to value self-discipline, an industrious approach and sticking up for what you believed in – skills that he subsequently put to good use for Gloucestershire in doggedly defending his wicket as if it were his most prized possession.

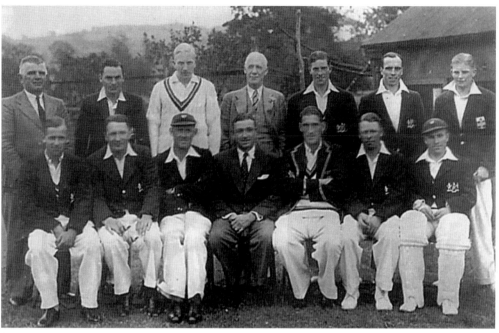

Gloucestershire team line-up, 1939 . Reg Sinfield is third from left in the front row, surrounded by many other Gloucestershire Greats..

After his brief naval career, Sinfield initially played in Minor County cricket for his native Hertfordshire before joining the Lord's ground-staff, and making his first-class debut for the MCC. Whilst at Lord's, his bowling impressed Charlie Parker, who recommended that he join Gloucestershire. Following a two-year qualification period, Sinfield became one of the County's most hardy cricketers and a great friend of the irascible Parker. The pair became inseparable, always travelling together to away games, with Sinfield being one of Parker's most loyal supporter.

He was also a good friend of Wally Hammond, to the extent of even developing an almost whimsical rapport with the master batsman. He certainly got on far better with Hammond than many of his team-mates, and when Hammond was County captain, he would often take Sinfield out into the middle to look at the wicket before the toss had been made and to share a few thoughts with his trusted ally. From time to time, the pair also opened the batting together, although as Sinfield later recalled 'Wally didn't much like the new ball. He would

tell me to take as much of the strike as I could until the shine had gone off the ball, and he'd give me a crafty look, reminding me I was more used to opening than he was!'

Sinfield also had a sharp and lively wit, and in 1926 after scoring his maiden Championship century, he politely asked Lt-Col. Robinson, the County's captain, if his feat at Taunton merited the award of his County cap. The captain replied that it would, but only if he could repeat the feat in the forthcoming match with Nottingham-shire, and in particular against Larwood and Voce. In typically gritty fashion, Sinfield responded with 124.

Even before war had been declared in 1939, Sinfield decided that it would be his final summer of County cricket, and he subsequently became an amiable and perceptive coach at Clifton College, and later Colston's School, where Chris Broad was amongst his charges. After retiring from the County game, Sinfield also took great pride in his garden at Ticken-ham, just down the road from his son's nursery business, and he also served as a dedicated church warden at the local parish church.

David Robert Smith

RHB & RM, 1956-1970

Born: 5 October 1934, Fishponds, Bristol

Batting

M	I	NO	Runs	Av
357	488	110	4640	12.27
40	28	12	165	10.31
50	100	ct/st		
6	-	282		
-	-	9		

Bowling

Balls	Runs	Wkts	Av	5wI	10wM
67191	27449	1159	23.68	48	6
1952	1211	52	23.29		

Best Performances

74 v MCC at Lord's, 1961
7-20 v Sussex at Stroud, 1962
45 v Surrey at The Oval, 1964
4-6 v Hampshire at Bristol, 1970

During his fifteen-year career, David Smith proved to be one of the most effective strike bowlers to ever play for Gloucestershire, taking over a hundred wickets on five occasions, in addition to winning five Test caps for England. Many good judges said that he also possessed the best natural bowling action in the country.

His distinguished cricketing career followed a brief period in professional football as an outside right with both Bristol City and Millwall. Indeed, whilst at school in Fishponds, Smith had preferred football to cricket and he won honours with the England Youth team.

After making his County debut in 1956, Smith won a regular place in the County side the following summer. During his first full season, he took 106 wickets and won his County cap. His pace and movement off the pitch surprised many County batsmen, especially as Smith had a short run-up to the wicket and a fast, whippy action. He was also able to swing the ball away from right-handed batsmen, and had excellent control of line plus several quite deceptive changes of pace.

Over the next few seasons, he became a most hostile new-ball partner to Tony Brown, and in 1959 Smith took 110 Championship wickets and was tipped by several shrewd judges as an England bowler of the future. At the time, though, he was still a professional footballer, but after playing one full season with Millwall in the Third Division, Smith hung up his football boots and concentrated on cricket.

It proved to be a wise move as he went on to capture 143 wickets in 1960, and his hostile bowling was a feature of Gloucestershire's three-wicket victory over the South Africans. The following winter, Smith toured New Zealand with the MCC team, and played in all three of the representative matches.

After a promising start to the 1961 season, he was drafted into the England squad for the Ashes series. In the end, he failed to make the final eleven, but he was included in the tour party for the visit to India and Pakistan in 1961/62, and played in all five Tests against India, on wickets that did not suit his type of bowling.

Throughout his career, Smith shouldered a heavy workload for Gloucestershire, and his eagerness to bowl for over after over was even more commendable given the fact that he was slightly asthmatic. In hindsight, it may have been that Smith was over-bowled, and his willingness to bowl long spells led to him picking up several injuries. In 1966, he missed the first two months of the season after a cartilage operation, and at the end of the 1970 season, having taken 66 wickets at a cost of 33, Smith retired from the County game after persistent knee and back injuries.

Harry Smith
RHB & WK, 1912-1935

Born: 21 May 1891, Fishponds, Bristol
Died: 12 November 1937, Downend, Bristol

Batting

M	I	NO	Runs	Av
393	645	55	13334	22.60
50	**100**	**ct/st**		
75	10	442/264		

Bowling

Balls	Runs	Wkts	Av	5wI	10wM
18	7	0	-	-	-

Best Performance
149 v Essex at Cheltenham, 1923

Harry Smith was Gloucestershire's regular wicketkeeper in the years either side of the First World War, and in 1928 he kept for England in the Lord's Test of the series against the West Indies. It was a worthy reward for the compact and courageous 'keeper, who often played with badly swollen fingers or cracked bones in his hands, with the bruises and double thumbnails bearing testimony to his bravery, which he modestly accepted with a wry smile on his face.

He began his career with Frenchay CC, as a forceful left-handed batsman and useful leg-spinner. His success with bat and ball led to his selection for Bristol Colts against the County side in 1911, but during the match the Colts wicketkeeper was injured and Smith took over. His glovework was so impressive that he was offered a trial with the County, and after proving to be a natural 'keeper, he was signed as understudy to Jack Board.

In 1912, Smith made his first-team debut against Nottinghamshire at Trent Bridge. At the time, he mixed his cricket career in the summer with life in the winter as a professional footballer. After some impressive performances as a winger in the local leagues, he joined the staff of Bristol Rovers, before accepting a contract with Bolton Wanderers. After the war, Smith won a regular place in the Gloucestershire side, and in the match against Hampshire at Southampton in 1919, he displayed his batting talents with scores of 120 and 102*.

In 1921, Smith passed the landmark of a thousand runs for the first time in his career, and in 1923 he established a new County record by dismissing six Sussex batsmen in an innings of their match at Bristol. By this time, he was regarded as one of the best professional 'keepers in the country, and during 1923 he kept wicket for the Players against the Gentlemen at Lord's.

Over the next few seasons, he continued to maintain a high standard of 'keeping, standing up to the likes of Goddard, Parker and Sinfield. A measure of his deft and efficient glovework was that he conceded just one bye in four consecutive innings during 1927. Lancashire's George Duckworth was still considered to be the best 'keeper in the country, but Smith's talents got their due reward in 1928 when he was drafted into the England side for the First Test against the West Indies at Lord's.

Smith fell ill with heart problems in 1932 and did not play at all that summer, or for the next two years. He was restored to health by 1935, when he returned to the County's side for 13 matches. However, this proved to be his swan-song, as he retired from the playing staff at the end of the summer and subsequently mixed running a pub in Downend with coaching duties at the County Ground. Smith had specific responsibility for the Colts side, but sadly, in November 1937, he contracted tubercular meningitis and died shortly afterwards.

Andrew Michael Smith
RHB & LM, 1991-present

Born: 1 October 1967, Dewsbury, Yorkshire

Batting

M	I	NO	Runs	Av
131	174	47	1590	12.52
202	96	57	433	11.10

50	100	ct/st
-	-	26
-	-	35

Bowling

Balls	Runs	Wkts	Av	5wI	10wM
22273	11060	456	24.25	20	5
9265	6200	231	26.84		

Best Performances
61 v Yorkshire at Gloucester, 1998
8-73 v Middlesex at Lord's, 1996
26* v Kent at Moreton-in-Marsh, 1996
6-39 v Hampshire at Southampton, 1995

Mike Smith was the best left-arm swing bowler in English cricket during the 1990s, yet despite being a consistent wicket-taker in Championship cricket, he only won a single Test cap – against the 1997 Australians at Headingley. It came during Smith's finest season in Championship cricket, but his Test debut proved to be a rather unhappy one. After struggling with injuries over the previous couple of seasons, it seems likely that Smith will remain a member of the one cap 'club'.

Smith's call-up to the England ranks at the end of July for the Fourth Test of the Ashes series was widely regarded in the West Country as being long overdue. Headingley had a reputation as a ground favouring swing bowling, and with Smith in fine form with the new ball, it seemed that the England selectors had chosen the right horse for the right course. This was partly due to Smith exploiting the conditions to return match figures of 10-132 in the Championship encounter with Yorkshire in the first week of June.

Smith was also in prime form, having just recorded his third ten-wicket haul of the summer with match figures of 10-106 against Derbyshire at Cheltenham. Events in the Headingley Test, however, did not turn out as Smith had hoped; in his third over he found the edge of Matthew Elliott's bat, only to see Graham Thorpe at first slip drop the relatively simple chance. Elliott was on

29 at the time, and went on to score 199 as Australia won by an innings to take a series lead. As *Wisden*'s correspondent observed, 'it was deemed by many observers to be the sort of dropped catch that costs a Test series.'

Smith remained wicket-less in his 23 overs, and later said that it was the only occasion during the summer that he had been unable to swing the ball. Had he been given the chance to operate with the new ball, it might have been very different, but it was no surprise that Smith was one of three players to lose their place for the Fifth Test. It was typical of the man that Smith returned to County cricket, and continued to be a prolific wicket-taker and one of the best new-ball bowlers in the land.

The Yorkshire-born Smith joined Gloucestershire in 1990, after impressing with the Combined Universities side in the B & H Cup. He quickly developed into a skiddy bowler, creating awkward lift and movement in the air, as well as having the knack of dismissing the best batsmen on good wickets. In 1995/96, he was chosen for the England A tour of Pakistan, but a rib injury forced him home after bowling just 22 overs. He has also become a key member of Gloucestershire's triumphant one-day side, delivering many economical spells, typified in 2000 by 4-27 in the semi-final of the Benson & Hedges Cup, plus 3-18 in the NatWest Trophy final.

Jeremy Nicholas Snape

RHB & OB, 1999-present

Born: 27 April 1973, Stoke-on-Trent, Staffs.

Batting

M	I	NO	Runs	Av
45	69	12	1946	34.14
72	62	11	1100	21.57

50	100	ct/st
12	3	26
3	1	27

Bowling

Balls	Runs	Wkts	Av	5wI	10wM
3220	1430	30	47.67	-	-
1532	1164	44	26.45	-	-

Best Performances

131 v Sussex at Cheltenham, 2001
3-27 v Durham at Chester-le-Street, 2001
104* v Nottinghamshire at Trent Bridge, 2001
4-27 v Worcestershire at Worcester, 1999

Not many English players, especially those of the past couple of decades, can proudly boast that they won the Man of the Match award on their international debut. But this is precisely what Jeremy Snape achieved, at the age of twenty-eight, when he played in England's One-Day International against Zimbabwe at Harare on 3 October 2001, during which he dismissed both of the Flower brothers in a tidy ten-over spell of off-spin and also took two fine catches.

Snape had an impressive sporting career at Denstone College and Durham University, leading England's Under-18 team on their tour to Canada in 1991, and being a member of the England Under-19 squad to Pakistan the following winter. Whilst at Durham, he was also selected in the Combined Universities team, and won the Gold Award after taking 3-34 in the Benson & Hedges match with Worcestershire.

In 1992, he made his debut for Northamptonshire, for whom he had played second-team cricket for several years. However, Snape subsequently failed to win a regular place in their Championship side, and played mainly in their one-day side. With Graeme Swann and Jason Brown establishing themselves, Snape decided to move and join Gloucestershire for 1999.

It was a rags-to-riches change, as he went from being a fringe player to an intrinsic member of the most successful one-day team in the country. He soon showed his all-round abilities to the Bristol supporters, as a sharp spinner of the ball with an intelligent change of pace, a fine fielder with a safe pair of hands, and a combative batsman who was not afraid to open his shoulders. Indeed, 1999 saw Snape make some telling contributions with the bat, often in tight finishes. He deservedly won the Gold Award in the Benson & Hedges Super Cup semi-final after a quick-fire half-century off just 41 balls had seen his team to a sizeable total, out of the range of Sussex's powerful batting line-up.

He played in each of Gloucestershire's winning sides in their four Lord's finals in 1999 and 2000, and he was a key member of the side that added the 2000 Norwich Union silverware to their overflowing trophy cabinet. Snape also delivered an accurate spell in the 2000 Benson & Hedges final that stifled Glamorgan's quest of a sizeable total. Then, after being part of the Gloucestershire side that won the NatWest Trophy, he celebrated the following day at Bristol, top-scoring with 71 in their season's best total of 269-9 in the day-night encounter with Leicestershire.

Snape continued to display his all-round talents in 2001, and during the summer hit four centuries – in the Championship against Derbyshire, Sussex and Nottinghamshire, plus an unbeaten 104 in Norwich Union game against Warwickshire.

Edward James Spry
RHB & LB, 1899-1921

Born: 31 July 1881, Bristol
Died: 18 November 1958, Knowle

Batting

M	I	NO	Runs	Av
89	154	24	1447	11.13
50	100	ct/st		
2	-	45		

Bowling

Balls	Runs	Wkts	Av	5wI	10wM
7150	4306	149	28.89	13	3

Best Performances
76 v Nottinghamshire at Trent Bridge, 1903
8-52 v Warwickshire at Bristol, 1903

Ted Spry had a strike-rate on a par with two of Gloucestershire's greatest spinners – Parker and Goddard – and during his career as a professional in the early 1900s, Spry claimed 149 wickets with his clever leg-spin.

His father, John Spry, was the groundsman at Nevil Road, so it was not surprising that young Ted soon took a keen interest in cricket. When the youngster was growing up, there was always someone around to pass on a few coaching tips, or a batsman to practise bowling at in the nets.

W.G. had a very high opinion of the youngster, but Grace had departed the County by August 1899, when Spry made his County debut against Warwickshire – on a wicket at Nevil Road that he had helped his father prepare! The young professional had a high, whirling action and after years of practice at the County Ground, he could impart considerable spin on the ball. Spry duly had an extended run in the side in 1902, which proved to be his most successful season, with a haul of 60 wickets at a cost of 21.66.

The following summer, he shone again with both bat and ball, recording two career-best performances within the space of a week in mid-July. Firstly, he took 8-52 on his home pitch against Warwickshire, and then seven days later against Nottinghamshire, Spry made an accomplished 76 in the space of two hours on a drying wicket at Trent Bridge. However, Spry's greatest moment that summer came in the match against London County at Crystal Palace when he caught and bowled W.G., albeit after the grand old man had scored 150, and returned figures of 5-67 against the doctor's side.

Spry had a few difficulties with his action in 1908 and a loss of confidence in 1909 meant that he met with little success. With the County suffering a dreadful season, Spry accepted an offer to play in the local leagues and he made no more appearances in the years leading up to the outbreak of the First World War.

He continued to live at the ground and subsequently took over the duties of groundsman from his father. Even after the First World War, he was still one of the most successful bowlers in Bristol club cricket, and in 1921 he returned to the Gloucestershire side to play as an amateur in one match. He continued to play in local leagues until 1929, and in later life he also served on the Gloucestershire CCC committee.

Javagal Srinath

RHB & RFM, 1995

Born: 31 August 1969, Mysore, India

Batting

M	I	NO	Runs	Av
15	24	4	314	15.70
15	12	3	36	4.00
50	100	ct/st		
-	-	5		
-	-	5		

Bowling

Balls	Runs	Wkts	Av	5wI	10wM
3412	1661	87	19.09	5	2
801	452	33	13.70		

Best Performances
44 v Kent at Canterbury, 1995
9-76 v Glamorgan at Abergavenny, 1995
11* v Durham at Chester-le-Street, 1995
4-33 v Combined Universities at Bristol, 1995

Javagal Srinath had a wonderful season as Gloucestershire's overseas player in 1995. The Indian took 87 wickets at just 19 runs apiece, and formed a highly effective new-ball partnership with left-armer Mike Smith – although it might never have happened, had Australian batsman David Boon not withdrawn after having agreed to join the County for 1995.

Srinath was an unknown quantity when he arrived in Britain, having been hired just for one year with Walsh on duty with the West Indies. By the end of the season, the Indian left nobody in doubt as to his abilities as a pace bowler, and would have taken over a hundred wickets had he not been affected by a combination of sheer fatigue and a virus towards the end of a highly successful summer.

The quietly spoken and popular quick bowler surprised many County batsmen with some deft changes of pace, twice taking ten wickets in a match – 10-97 against Yorkshire at Middlesborough, plus 13-150 against Glamorgan at Abergavenny. It was in this game on the shirt-front wicket at Avenue Road that the shrewd Indian displayed his wiles, carefully bowling within himself and varying his pace, whilst all around him other bowlers were being hit to all parts of the ground. A total of 1,559 runs were scored, yet in Glamorgan's second innings, Srinath returned career-best figures of 9-76 from 21 astute overs of seam bowling.

The pace bowler from Karnataka made his Test debut in 1990/91, and for a while he received guidance on the art of pace bowling from Dennis Lillee at his academy in Madras. However, Srinath freely admits that this summer with Gloucestershire was the turning point in his career, and despite the wise words from Lillee, it was while he was with Gloucestershire that he really learnt how to bowl on a variety of pitches. The lessons he learnt with the West Country side have been subsequently put to practice on Test arenas all over the world, and with his smooth action, the 'Karnataka Express' has extracted movement and unexpected lift from the most docile of surfaces.

Since Kapil Dev's retirement in 1994/95, Srinath has emerged as the spearhead of the Indian attack. He has amply filled the void left by the great man's retirement, and has become adept at making the initial breakthrough with the new ball, before returning later in the innings to mop up the tail.

Statistics never tell the full story, but in the case of Srinath's Test career, there is an exception. A large percentage of his Test wickets have been taken outside India, on fast, bouncy tracks in Australia and South Africa, or on green wickets in England. This confirms how Srinath has quickly learnt to adapt his bowling to different conditions, and pitches very different to those he was brought up on in Mysore.

Andrew Willis Stovold ────────────────
RHB & WK, 1973-1990

Born: 19 March 1953, Southmead, Bristol

Batting

M	I	NO	Runs	Av
346	617	35	17460	30.00
290	281	32	7081	28.44
50	100	ct/st		
97	20	268/44		
35	4	141/21		

Bowling

Balls	Runs	Wkts	Av	5wI	10wM
309	218	4	54.50	-	-

Best Performances

212* v Northamptonshire at Northampton, 1982
1-0 v Derbyshire at Bristol, 1976
123 v Combined Universities at Oxford, 1982

Andy Stovold won the Gold Award when Gloucestershire won the Benson & Hedges Cup in 1977. Right from the outset, the stocky right-hander played some imperious strokes, with a series of forcing shots off the back foot, plus his trademark cut, square of the wicket.

In typically assertive fashion, his cavalier efforts never let the Kent bowlers settle, and his innings of 71 was part of a quick-fire opening partnership of 79 with Sadiq Mohammad that laid the foundations of Gloucestershire's decent total. Then, when his side where in the field, Stovold held three fine catches behind the stumps as the County won the trophy for the first time in their history.

He had been an outstanding wicketkeeper-batsman since his days as a schoolboy at Filton High School when, as Andrew Willis-Stovold, he won honours with the Gloucestershire Schools side. He also won selection for the England Under-15 team, before playing in the England Under-19 side and touring India and the West Indies with the English Young Cricketers.

He made his debut for Gloucestershire during the 1973 Cheltenham Festival, and despite winning selection as a batsman, he deputised behind the stumps when Roy Swetman was injured. Stovold's abilities behind the stumps, and his prowess as a hard-hitting batsman subsequently won him a

regular place, and Stovold was in the County's side for the nerve-jangling Gillette Cup semi-final at Worcester and the final against Sussex, which Gloucestershire won by 40 runs.

In 1974, he scored his maiden Championship hundred against Derbyshire at Cheltenham, before going out to South Africa, where he played for two seasons for Orange Free State in the Currie Cup, in addition to coaching at Wynberg Boys High School. In 1976, Stovold passed a thousand runs for the first time in his career and won his County cap. He also came close to adding an England one, after narrowly missing out on a place as the reserve 'keeper on the MCC winter tour.

The signing of wicketkeepers Andy Brassington and then Jack Russell allowed 'Stov' to concentrate on his role as an opening batsman. It proved to be a wise decision, as in 1981 he hit a career best 212* against Northamptonshire, followed by 181 against Derbyshire and 122 against Surrey at the start of the 1983 season.

Andy enjoyed a benefit year in 1987 before retiring at the end of the 1990 season. For several winters he had been a geography and PE teacher at Tockington Manor prep school, but he subsequently moved back into cricket as a coach and mentor for Gloucestershire's Second XI. His sons, Neil and Nicholas, have both played for the County's Second XI, whilst his brother, Martin, also played for Gloucestershire between 1979 and 1982.

Andrew Symonds
RHB & RM/OB, 1995-1996

Born: 9 June 1975, Birmingham

Batting
M	I	NO	Runs	Av
36	61	6	2535	46.09
45	44	2	1213	28.88

50	100	ct/st
13	7	17
7	-	22

Bowling
Balls	Runs	Wkts	Av	5wI	10wM
939	474	13	36.46	-	-
438	364	14	26.00		

Best Performances
254* v Glamorgan at Abergavenny, 1995
2-21 v Northamptonshire at Bristol, 1996
95 v Combined Universities at Bristol, 1995
3-34 v Essex at Colchester, 1996

Andrew Symonds had a phenomenal first season in County cricket in 1995, with the twenty-year-old Anglo-Australian hitting the headlines with a remarkable 254* against Glamorgan as he became the County's youngest ever double centurion, and all whilst creating a new world record with 16 sixes in his explosive innings.

Symonds' feats came at Abergavenny, one of the most delightful and picturesque of all the grounds on the County circuit, but certainly not one with the longest boundaries. Even so, many of Symonds' sledgehammer blows would have been sixes on the largest Test arena, with his record-breaking sixteenth six sailing high over the neatly mown outfield, over a row of hawthorns and into tennis courts on an adjoining recreation ground.

The young tyro had arrived at the crease with his side on 73-5, but he proceeded to take the game by the scruff of the neck, sharing a partnership of 213 with reserve wicketkeeper Reggie Williams and hitting 22 fours to add to his 16 sixes. Gloucestershire finished on 461, but this was not the end of Symonds' big hitting, as in the second innings he added another four sixes to take his tally to 20, and past the previous record of 17 set by Warwickshire's Jim Stewart in 1959.

He also recorded Championship centuries against Surrey at The Oval, Somerset at

Taunton and Essex at Cheltenham, as well as many playing some enterprising innings in limited-overs games, when some of his blows bordered on the daring. His efforts resulted in Symonds being voted as the country's young Player of the Year. At the same time, pressure was being applied, some felt unfairly, on the twenty year old to declare himself as being England-qualified. Despite being born in Birmingham, Symonds' family had moved to Australia when he was eighteen months old, and he had been brought up in Queensland. Much debate took place during the course of 1995 about his nationality, given his dual qualification. In an attempt to force things, Symonds was selected in the England 'A' team, but he declined the offer and opted instead to seek selection for Australia, his adopted country.

Symonds had already attended the Australian Cricket Academy in 1993/94, and was a regular in the Queensland side, scoring a century for them against England on the 1994/95 Ashes tour. However, he had still not yet played in representative cricket for Australia, so he was able to return to Gloucestershire in 1996 and play alongside Courtney Walsh, the County's overseas player and captain. Once again, Symonds passed a thousand in all first-class games and was awarded his County cap. He struck two Championship centuries, including a pulsating 127 off 107 balls against Warwickshire at Cheltenham and that saw his side to an innings victory.

Christopher Glyn Taylor

RHB & OB, 2000-present

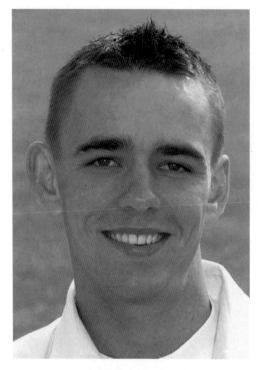

Born: 27 September 1976, Bristol

Batting

M	I	NO	Runs	Av
23	40	2	1406	37.00
43	34	7	425	15.74

50	100	ct/st
4	4	13
1	-	15

Bowling

Balls	Runs	Wkts	Av	5wI	10wM
165	136	3	45.33	-	-

Best Performances

196 v Nottinghamshire at Trent Bridge, 2001
3-126 v Northamptonshire at Cheltenham, 2000
63 v Northamptonshire at Cheltenham, 2001*

In 2000, Chris Taylor had a dream debut for Gloucestershire, scoring 104 against Middlesex at Lord's to become the first ever batsman to score a debut hundred in Championship cricket on the hallowed turf at the headquarters of English cricket. The twenty-four year old was also the first ever batsman to score a Championship hundred for Gloucestershire on his first-class debut. If the critics are right (and they invariably are), Taylor could be the next in a long line of illustrious Gloucestershire batsmen to have a highly productive career at County level and to play for England.

From an early age, Taylor has had a liking for large scores. Whilst at Colston's School in Bristol, he scored 278* and a series of impressive innings led to his selection for the England Schools Under-18 team. His alert and razor-sharp fielding also led to the schoolboy winning the Cricket Society's A.A. Thomson's Fielding Prize. In 1998, Taylor made his debut for Gloucestershire Second XI, and he continued in prolific vein in 1999, hitting an unbeaten 300 in the match against Somerset Second XI – the third highest individual score in Second XI history.

2000 saw the diminutive cricketer make his record-breaking debut, and also receive a fair amount of sledging from the hard-nosed opponents who could not quite believe that the batsman, with the looks and frame of a schoolboy, could unfurl so many powerful and crisply-timed shots against the seasoned professionals. Taylor did not rise to the bait, and instead let his bat do the talking. He had also come to the crease in the twelfth over, with the scoreboard reading 29-4, but he was not put off by this situation and remained calm and composed in making a maiden century off 184 balls, with 14 boundaries.

The 2001 season saw Taylor consolidate this fine start to his first-class career. He impressed many people with his graceful and relaxed batting, as well as his swift fielding – especially in one-day games, where he has shone in the outfield, swiftly patrolling the boundary boards and belying his slight frame by returning the ball with powerful and accurate throws. In particular, he put the Nottinghamshire bowlers to the sword, with 196 against them at Trent Bridge at Bristol in June, followed by 148 in the return match in August. Sandwiched in between was a classy 140 off the Sussex attack at Cheltenham, and Gloucestershire supporters can look forward to further fine innings from this most talented young batsman.

Charles Lucas Townsend
LHB & OB, 1893-1922

Born: 7 November 1876, Clifton
Died: 17 October 1958, Stockton-on-Tees

Batting

M	I	NO	Runs	Av
161	275	19	7754	30.28
50	100	ct/st		
29	19	162		

Bowling

Balls	Runs	Wkts	Av	5wI	10wM
26082	14326	655	21.87	64	18

Best Performances
224 v Essex at Clifton, 1899
9-48 v Middlesex at Lord's, 1898

Charles Townsend was the first and only bowler in cricket history to take a hat-trick in which all three victims were stumped. His unique feat occurred at Cheltenham in 1893 during Gloucestershire's match against Somerset, and all with the assistance of William Brain, who was later to become Glamorgan's regular wicket-keeper.

However, what made Townsend's feat even more remarkable was that at the time he was a callow youth of sixteen, and was playing in only his second first-class match. It was no flash in the pan either, as during three seasons in the First XI at Clifton College, the schoolboy leg-spinner took 199 wickets at a fraction over 10 runs apiece. It is no surprise then, that in the minds of many people, Townsend is the finest cricketer the famous college has ever produced.

Townsend had another claim to fame, as he was the godson of W.G., with whom his father Frank, a dependable batsman, had played in Gloucestershire's inaugural fixture in 1870 against Surrey. For several years, the doctor had been keeping an eye on his young godson, who as a fourteen year old took 10-68 against the College in their annual match against Knowle Park. W.G. had every confidence that the young leg-spinner would one day make his mark for the County, but even the 'Old Man' could not have forecast Townsend's meteoric rise in first-class cricket.

In 1895, Townend took no fewer than 131 wickets for the County, despite having been at Clifton until mid-July. During August, the tall leg-spinner claimed 94 wickets, bowling his leg-spinners at a brisk pace and extracting sharp spin to deceive even the most experienced of County batsmen. So successful was the lean and lanky youngster that he frequently opened the bowling, and found the hard, new ball ideal for his delivery that skidded straight on.

In the match against Nottinghamshire at Trent Bridge, Townsend returned figures of 16-122 which at the time were the second best in the County's history, and bettered only by W.G.'s 17-89 in the corresponding fixture at Cheltenham in 1877. The Nottinghamshire batsmen were in trouble against Townsend in the return game at Cheltenham, as the young spinner came close to emulating the doctor's achievement, finishing the game with 13-110. Just for good measure, he also added 12-wicket hauls in the matches with Sussex, Surrey and Somerset.

Townsend was also a graceful left-handed batsman, and in 1895 he shared a partnership of 223 with W.G. for the third wicket against Somerset at Bristol, during which Grace recorded his one hundredth century. Despite his relative inexperience, Townsend matched the doctor stroke for stroke, and he was at the wicket when Grace clipped Sammy Woods for four to reach the coveted landmark.

Townsend continued in a rich vein with both bat and ball in the next few seasons, claiming 113 wickets in 1896, while in 1897 he

took 92 wickets and recorded his maiden century against Yorkshire. The following year, he consolidated these achievements by recording the 'Double', with 1,270 runs and 145 wickets. He also took great delight in beating W.G.'s record for the best bowling figures in an innings for the County, taking 9-48 against Middlesex at Lord's. During 1898 he also took 9-128 against Warwickshire at Cheltenham, and in the return match at Edgbaston he claimed 10 wickets, and scored 139. After such grand all-round performances, the young player was one of *Wisden's* Five Cricketers of the Year.

Townsend did the Double again in 1899, this time scoring 2,440 runs and taking 101 wickets as he continued to confound opponents with both bat and ball. During another wonderful summer, he scored 224* against Essex on his old stamping ground at Clifton College and he appeared for the Gentlemen against the Players, in addition to making his England debut at Lord's in the Second Test of the series against Australia.

Although he claimed three wickets, England slumped to a ten-wicket defeat and Townsend did not play again until the Fifth Test at The Oval, after having smashed the tourists, bowling for an unbeaten 135* in their game with Gloucestershire during the Cheltenham Festival.

The year 1900 proved to be his final full season of County cricket, as he started to pursue a legal career, acting initially as a solicitor and later as Official Receiver at Stockton-on-Tees. He still made an occasional appearance for Gloucestershire, and remained close friends with many of the Gloucestershire players, including W.G., for whom he acted as solicitor. In May 1902, he assembled an eleven to play Grace's London County side at Bristol in aid of the NSPCC Appeal.

In his brief appearances, he showed that he was still capable of taking an attack apart. An example occurred in 1906, when he returned to the County side for the match with Worcestershire, and despite a lack of match practice, Townsend hit an imperious 214 in his first innings of the summer. Batting at number three, he had arrived at the crease with the score on a precarious 1-1, but by the time he was dismissed, Gloucestershire had moved on to 421-5.

In 1909, he also returned to the County side for the match against the Australians at Cheltenham, and he delighted the large Festival crowd with a truly wonderful 129 in just two hours. He also made a few appearances after the First World War, including the match in 1920 against Somerset on the Fry's ground. Gloucestershire were set 274 to win on the final afternoon – on paper, this was quite a daunting target given that they had been dismissed for just 22 in their first innings. But Townsend turned the tables on Somerset, scoring 84 out of 119 in just 75 minutes as Gloucestershire raced to a four-wicket win.

Born: 16 October 1869, Meerut, India
Died: 14 December 1940, Isleworth

Batting

M	I	NO	Runs	Av
80	135	13	3252	26.65

50	100	ct/st		
12	7	26		

Bowling

Balls	Runs	Wkts	Av	5wI	10wM
8	4	0	-	-	-

Best Performance
180 v Nottinghamshire at Bristol, 1898

Major Walter Troup was a steady batsman who opened the batting on many occasions with W.G. Grace in the 1880s and 1890s. He subsequently became a good friend of the doctor and stepped into the breach in 1899 to captain the County after W.G. dramatically ceased his connection with Gloucestershire.

However, Troup was only in office for one year before returning to India, where he was a police officer, subsequently rising to the rank of chief of police in Poona and the North West Provinces. Even so, he regularly arranged time off to return to the UK during the summer months and played for the County until 1911.

Sometimes he had to collude with W.G. in order to obtain sick leave and see out the rest of the season with the County side. On one occasion in mid-summer, he was due to return to India, so he went to see W.G. to seek his advice. 'Fetch me a pen, ink and some paper. I'll soon settle it,' said the doctor, who then wrote a letter stating that Troup was in a quite low state of health, and needed plenty of outdoor exercise, preferably cricket. Troup duly remained with Gloucestershire for the rest of the summer, and his runs were literally what the doctor had ordered!

The son of a general in the Indian Army, Troup was an outstanding schoolboy sportsman, representing Cheltenham College and Gloucestershire at cricket, hockey and rugby, and he made his debut in the Gloucestershire XI in 1887 at the tender age of seventeen.

At first, Troup was a rather painstaking and defensive batsman, who on more than one occasion batted for over an hour without scoring. In fact, in the match against Lancashire at Liverpool in 1888, the youngster patiently remained on nought for 95 minutes before being stumped. He was also out leg before in the second innings without scoring, to record one of the longest pairs on record!

As he matured and became more experienced, he became a more fluent stroke-maker, and in 1898 he hit four centuries – 176 against Somerset at Bristol, 127 against the same opponents at Taunton, 100 against Essex at Clifton, plus a career-best 180 against Nottinghamshire at Bristol. His tally for the season of 968 runs was only exceeded by Townsend and W.G., and *Wisden* commented that 'Next to his captain, he was the most dependable batsman in the team. Troup added enormously to the strength of the Gloucestershire batting, and he had a great share in the advance made by the County.'

If Troup had resided on a permanent basis in Gloucestershire, he could have been one of the County's finest batsmen of the Edwardian era.

Courtney Andrew Walsh
RHB & RF, 1984-1998

Born: 30 October 1962, Kingston, Jamaica

Batting

M	I	NO	Runs	Av
184	237	57	2581	14.33
173	107	23	835	9.94

50	100	ct/st
7	-	52
-	-	29

Bowling

Balls	Runs	Wkts	Av	5wI	10wM
36168	17390	869	20.01	61	15
8012	5112	243	21.04		

Best Performances
66 v Kent at Cheltenham, 1994
9-72 v Somerset at Bristol, 1986
38 v Derbyshire at Derby, 1996
6-21 v Kent at Bristol, 1990
6-21 v Cheshire at Bristol, 1992

If asked to name the finest overseas player ever to represent Gloucestershire, many of the County's supporters would opt for Courtney Walsh, the lion-hearted fast bowler and loyal servant to the West Country side from 1984 until 1998. In 1986, he took 118 wickets at just 18 runs apiece, and he was still as effective in 1998, claiming 106 victims.

The tall, slim and languid Jamaican was recommended to the County by Tom Graveney, and in 1984 he made his debut for Gloucestershire before joining the West Indies team on their tour of England. The following year, he made an immediate impact in his first full season with the County, taking 85 wickets and forming a very effective, and at times quite frightening, pace attack with David Lawrence, helping the club move no less than fourteen places up the table.

1986 saw Walsh become the country's leading wicket-taker, reaching the 100-wicket mark on 9 August – earlier than anyone since Warwickshire's Lance Gibbs in 1971. Had rain not interrupted them, Gloucestershire might have become County Champions, as Walsh heroically spearheaded their attack, bowling with great hostility to produce a string of match-winning performances. Amongst the highlights were twelve wickets in the home and away wins over Hampshire, plus eleven in the demolition of Surrey at Bristol, and he was a

fitting choice as one of *Wisden*'s Five Cricketers of the Year.

Despite a year-round workload and regular appearances for the West Indies in Tests and One-Day Internationals, he continued to spearhead the West Country attack in the late 1980s and early 1990s. Year in, year out, Walsh bowled his heart out for the County, producing a number of spells that more than justified David Graveney's comment that Walsh was 'the best old-ball bowler in the country'. The only spat with the County came at the end of his illustrious career, when there was much confusion as the County decided that Walsh's services should not be retained. Walsh responded with an open letter to his Gloucestershire supporters, explaining his side of the contractual wranglings, just in case they thought that he was deserting them.

In his youth, Walsh had been capable of bowling very fast, but as he matured into one of the great West Indian bowlers, he cut his run down to 13 or 14 paces. Unlike other members of the Caribbean pace attack, he made sparing use of the bouncer, with his shorter ball threatening the batsman's ribcage and frequently resulting in them fending the ball off glove or splice into the hands of the fielder crouching at short-leg. Rather than relying on sheer pace, Walsh developed subtle changes in speed, line, and length, and so adept was he at disguising his intentions that not even his Gloucestershire team-mates could predict at what pace the ball was likely to come out of his hand.

A combination of durability, stamina, strong character and sheer class allowed Walsh to develop into one of the most successful bowlers of the modern age, and his determination to succeed helped him overcome several injuries that might have stopped the career of less tenacious men. His modest and affable personality, to say nothing of his success with the ball, made him an ideal team man. He also had several spells as the County's captain, initially taking over in 1993, when Tony Wright stood down as captain. He led Gloucestershire in 1994 and again in 1996, before handing over the reins to Mark Alleyne.

He had modest pretensions with the bat, and the sight of Courtney elaborately taking guard seemed almost more in keeping with a pantomime. Whilst many of his innings did end very quickly, Walsh could be a fierce hitter of the ball when he actually made contact. In a Sunday League game with Glamorgan in 1987, one of his sixes sailed through the glass window of the Radio Wales commentary box, sending its inhabitants diving for cover.

After enjoying great success during the 1980s with his countrymen, the 1990s steadily saw more downs than ups in the world of West Indies cricket. Although many of his colleagues departed the scene, Walsh battled through these difficult times, and continued to enjoy his cricket, fittingly becoming the all-time leading Test wicket-taker on his home ground at Sabina Park in the series with Zimbabwe. It was a wonderful achievement, and one that saw the Jamaican government honour Walsh with a motorcade around Kingston. It started off at Sabina Park, then went to his old school, Excelsior HS, and finished up at the Melbourne CC club ground, before a grand party at Jamaica House in honour of one of the Caribbean's finest servants.

In April 2001, he eventually called it a day, and brought the curtain down on his distinguished career, at the Sabina Park ground in the Fifth Test of the series with South Africa. Amongst emotional scenes, he bowed out of cricket with 519 Test wickets, and crowned his final game by helping his side to a 130 run victory. As Tony Becca, the West Indian journalist, wrote in a lengthy tribute to Courtney, 'Walsh deserved every cheer, every

handclap, every handshake, every word of congratulations. Walsh, however, is more than a great bowler. Despite his greatness, Walsh has never been too big or too tired to represent Jamaica or his club. He is always willing to sign autographs. Whenever he is at home, he often turns up at his club, trains with the youngsters and passes on tips. He never forgets those who, be it teachers, club members or friends, contributed to his development; and that is a testimony to his character and his personality – to his quality as a person. Courtney Walsh is loved everywhere he has played the game, not only because he is a great bowler, but because he is also a nice person. It is one thing to be a great performer; it is something else to be loved and adored.' Sentiments with which Gloucestershire fans would warmly agree.

Brian Douglas 'Bomber' Wells
RHB & OB, 1951-1959

Born: 27 July 1930, Gloucester

Batting

M	I	NO	Runs	Av
141	191	35	1041	6.67
50	100	ct/st		
-	-	66		

Bowling

Balls	Runs	Wkts	Av	5wI	10wM
32200	11524	544	21.18	29	5

Best Performances
42* v Glamorgan at Cheltenham, 1955
8-31 v Somerset at Taunton, 1953

'Bomber' Wells was one of the great characters of post-war Gloucestershire cricket. Despite moving to play for Notttinghamshire in 1960, the perky off-spinner remained very much a Gloucestershire man and has returned to live in the West Country and become a shrewd and passionate observer of the affairs of the County side.

The stocky, bespectacled spinner was the jovial and incorrigible jester in the County side from 1953 until 1959, with his bucolic wit and sheer love of the game enlightening many dark moments. Thickset and strongly built, his run-up usually consisted of a couple of short hops, before a quick whirl of the arms, almost taking the batsman by surprise.

He certainly imparted sharp spin on the ball, and together with a clever change of pace, teasing flight and well-concealed leg-break, Bomber was a handful on a dry and dusty wicket. As befitted his cheery outlook on life, he was also a cavalier tailender, and an innings from Wells was usually interspersed with lusty attempts to gleefully hit the ball higher than it had ever been hit before.

If this was not enough entertainment, his calling, or lack of it, would enliven proceedings, although his partners were often driven to distraction by his optimistic calls. One memorable example occurred during a partnership with Sam Cook, when both parties were nearly run out on several occasions. But survive they did, although Cook was clearly getting irritated by the near misses. After another

near fatal call, he yelled at Wells, 'For God's sake Bomber, call,' to which the irrepressible spinner shouted 'Tails!'

Born in Gloucester, he listened at a young age to his father and uncles sitting in front of the fire at their home in New Street, discussing the merits of the Gloucestershire side. Like so many other young boys of his generation, he gleefully batted and bowled in impromptu games in the street, as well as in the playground at Linden Road school and later on the outfield of the Spa Ground.

After leaving school and starting an apprenticeship as a printer, Bomber began playing in organised matches for various clubs before graduating to Gloucester City. As he approached the end of his apprenticeship, he had few thoughts of ever playing County cricket, but in 1951 he was drafted into the County side when Goddard was taken ill and Sam Cook had damaged his hand whilst fielding. Wells celebrated his call-up with 6-47.

He subsequently became a full-time member of the County's staff, alongside fellow spinner John Mortimore and later David Allen. Although Bomber's wickets came at a cheaper cost, Mortimore and Allen were superior batsmen and more agile fielders. After leading Gloucestershire Second XI to the Second Eleven Championship in 1959, Bomber joined Nottinghamshire, and in his first season took 120 wickets. He remained with them until the mid-1960s, by which time his career tally had reached 999. It was typical of the man that he promptly retired, saying 'plenty of bowlers have taken a thousand or more wickets in their career, but none have ever taken 999!'

Sir Philip Francis Cunningham Williams

RHB, 1919-1925

Born: 6 July 1884, Kensington, London
Died: 6 May 1958, Westminster, London

Batting

M	I	NO	Runs	Av
112	198	10	3081	16.38
50	100	ct/st		
16	-	45		

Bowling

Balls	Runs	Wkts	Av	5wI	10wM
168	173	2	86.50	-	-

Best Performances

87 v Leicestershire at Leicester, 1919
1-0 v Worcestershire at Worcester, 1919

Sir Philip Francis Cunningham Williams hailed from the Dorset landed gentry, and in 1949 he was High Sheriff of Dorset. The Old Etonian had captained Gloucestershire in 1923, as well as in the 1930s serving on the working party that oversaw the acquisition of the Fry's ground. However, before the First World War, he also came quite close to playing for an England side despite having played no first-class cricket.

Williams was a free-scoring batsman at Eton, but after going up to Trinity College, he failed to force his way into the Oxford side and win a blue. After graduating, Williams accepted an offer to spend a year working in New Zealand, and little did he realise that his journey out to New Zealand almost resulted in him playing in a representative match for an English XI.

During the winter of 1906/07, the MCC had sent an all-amateur side out to New Zealand for a seventeen-match tour which culminated in two unofficial 'Tests'. Early in the tour, the captain Wynyard snapped a tendon in his right leg, so when two other members of the tour picked up strains, Williams gleefully answered an appeal to play for the MCC against a XVIII of West Coast, and a XV of Nelson and Marlborough.

Further injuries led to his call-up again later in the tour for the match against XV of Wairarapa and then, with the First 'Test' approaching, Williams made his first-class debut for the MCC against Hawkes Bay at Napier. Unfortunately, he only made 3, and the injured

players had recovered enough to play in the 'Tests', but had Williams met with more success with the bat, he might easily have made a dramatic and quite unexpected entry into representative cricket.

He returned soon afterwards to the UK, and entered the banking world, but he still found enough time to continue playing for Dorset in the Minor County Championship, as well as for the MCC and various wandering elevens.

After the First World War, he agreed to turn out for Gloucestershire, and he made his County debut in 1919. In 1923, he took over the captaincy, and helped the club rise from thirteenth to eleventh place in the County table. However, his work commitments prevented him from continuing the following year, and he handed over the leadership to Douglas Robinson.

He subsequently only played occasionally for Gloucestershire and despite retiring from the playing side of the game in 1925, he remained an active figure behind-the-scenes. In the winter of 1932/33, he acted as one of the co-directors of the Gloucestershire CCC Ground Company Ltd that purchased the Fry's ground and helped to create a base for the Gloucestershire nursery.

Arthur Edward Wilson

LHB & WK, 1936-1955

Born: 18 May 1910, Paddington, London

Batting

M	I	NO	Runs	Av
318	486	73	10532	25.50

50	100	ct/st		
58	7	416/169		

Bowling

Balls	Runs	Wkts	Av	5wl	10wM
2	1	0	-	-	-

Best Performance

188 v Sussex at Chichester, 1949

Andy Wilson was Gloucestershire's wicketkeeper in the years either side of the Second World War. He was a highly reliable wicketkeeper, with the mental strength and physical courage to 'keep in a way that was unobtrusive to the County's fine spinners, especially Tom Goddard. The great off-spinner would regularly make the ball turn and lift alarmingly from off to leg, but, time and again, Wilson would move deftly across to pouch the ball or snaffle any faint edge.

'Keeping on the dry wickets, or at Bristol with its low, slow bounce, was a daunting prospect, but Wilson made it look the easiest job in the world. Even in the twilight years of his career in the 1950s, he had few peers behind the stumps, and in 1953 at Portsmouth he created a new County record by taking ten catches in the match against Hampshire.

Wilson had joined the MCC groundstaff in 1932, after success as a left-arm spinner with North Wembley CC. He subsequently played alongside Denis Compton and George Emmett for the Young Professionals and helped out in the nets, and it was here that the MCC secretary spotted Wilson's abilities as he was 'keeping for fun in the nets.

As luck would have it, the following year the regular Middlesex 'keeper Fred Price was injured before the start of the away match with Gloucestershire, and Wilson was hurriedly called to Bristol to make his first-class debut. For the next couple of years, he remained on the fringe of the Middlesex team, and helped their Second XI to the Minor County title in 1935.

With the retirement of Harry Smith, he wrote to Gloucestershire, asking if they would engage him as their wicketkeeper. They answered in the affirma-

tive, and Wilson moved to the West Country in 1936. However, he had to spend two years qualifying by residence before he could play in the Championship. Therefore, he had to make do with playing in the odd friendly, plus club cricket for Gloucester and the Stinchcombe Stragglers, whilst Bert Watkins and Vic Hopkins filled in behind the timbers.

From 1938 until 1955, Wilson was the County's first-choice 'keeper, and he also developed into a most dependable left-handed batsman, playing many valiant innings, and coming good just when runs were most needed. He celebrated his first full season by hitting 1,138 runs, and he also made 130 against his former employers at Lord's during a stand of 192 with Billy Neale – and all whilst wearing a Middlesex Second XI cap! Wilson's pugnacious batting and sound 'keeping also won him a place in the South team against the North. There was even talk of Wilson winning a place in a Test Trial, but this was the closest he ever came to representative honours.

During 1938, Wilson also shared in a record eighth-wicket partnership for Gloucestershire, adding 239 with Wally Hammond against Lancashire at Bristol. Wilson continued to be a consistent run-scorer after the war, 1947 being his most productive year as he amassed 1, 294 runs.

After retiring, Wilson went into journalism and worked for many years on the *Dursley Gazette*. He maintained a close involvement with the County as a member of their cricket committee and chairman of the Gloucester region. He remained very proud of his achievements on the field, and his association with so many great names.

Graham George Morley Wiltshire

RHB & RM, 1953-1960

Born: 16 April 1931, Chipping Sodbury

Batting

M	I	NO	Runs	Av
19	30	4	218	8.38
50	100	ct/st		
-	-	3		

Bowling

Balls	Runs	Wkts	Av	5wI	10wM
1813	835	25	33.40	1	-

Best Performances
39 v Derbyshire at Bristol, 1958
7-52 v Yorkshire at Headingley, 1958

The statistics above would suggest that Graham Wiltshire's contribution to Gloucestershire cricket is quite a modest one, and not worthy of inclusion as a 'Glorious Gloster'. But nothing could be further from the truth, as the fast medium bowler from Chipping Sodbury gave over forty loyal years of service to the County, starting as a player in the 1950s, and then from 1962 he served as the County's shrewd coach.

During this time, he gently groomed the talents of many of the County's finest home-grown players, and cheerfully oversaw the emergence of a host of good young cricketer. As Grahame Parker once wrote, Wiltshire was 'the Pied Piper for the Gloucestershire Young Cricketers, leading them out onto the long road of County cricket. Humorously articulate and dedicated to the cause, as the years progressed he developed a wonderfully perceptive appreci-ation of an individual cricketer's technical problems.'

Amongst the many fine players he nurtured were Jim Foat, David Graveney, and Andy Stovold, whilst Geoff Howarth, later of Surrey and New Zealand, and Roland Butcher of Middlesex and England also spent a formative period under Graham's guidance.

During the winter months, Wiltshire visited many schools throughout the county on the look out for the next generation of Gloucestershire cricketers. Then in the summer, besides hours of coaching, he would venture on quite lengthy scouting missions to watch promising young players in Minor County and youth cricket. The elevation of the likes of Devonians Jack Davey and John Childs and Andy Brassington from Staffordshire into the Gloucestershire side bore rich testament to Wiltshire's astute judgement and ability to spot a future County player.

It was also Wiltshire who was responsible for both Mike Procter and Barry Richards being attached to the County club in 1965. Both players had highly successful tours with the South African schoolboys' side in 1963. After impressing Wiltshire with their all-round abilities, he organised for both to be invited to Bristol in 1965, where they played in club cricket as well as in the County's Second XI, and also made an appearance for the first team against the touring Springboks.

Wiltshire joined the County's staff in 1952, but he only played occasionally between 1953 and 1960. The highlight of his playing career undoubtedly came at Headingley in June 1958, when he took a hat-trick against Yorkshire, dismissing Jimmy Binks, Mel Ryan and Mick Cowan to return career-best figures of 7-52.

Born: 25 September 1942, Clifton

Batting

M	I	NO	Runs	Av
98	158	27	1953	14.90
7	7	0	68	9.71

50	100	ct/st
4	-	31
-	-	1

Bowling

Balls	Runs	Wkts	Av	5wI	10wM
11509	4923	184	26.75	6	-
318	211	7	30.14		

Best Performances

74 v Hampshire at Bristol, 1965
8-78 v West Indians at Bristol, 1966
32 v Sussex at Moreton-in-Marsh, 1974
3-28 v Northamptonshire at Bristol, 1965

After Ken and David Graveney, Tony and Matt Windows are probably the most successful father and son combination in the history of Gloucestershire CCC.

Had he not opted to pursue a legal career, Tony Windows might have become one of the club's finest all-rounders. Indeed, after winning three blues at Cambridge in the early 1960s and winning a regular place in the Gloucestershire side, his potential was recognised by the MCC selectors, who selected Windows in their party of young cricketers to tour Pakistan in 1966/67.

He joined County colleague Mike Bissex and Mike Brearley, his friend from Cambridge days, who was leading the MCC's party of Under-25 cricketers to the sub-continent. However, Windows got few opportunities on the tour and did not play in any of the representative matches, but he did hit a brisk half-century at Chittagong against the East Pakistan's Governor's XI.

His selection for the tour was the result of an impressive start to his County career, and a productive season in 1966 during which his brisk out-swing bowling had demolished the West Indian batting in the first innings of the tour game at Bristol. He took seven consecutive wickets in an inspired spell of twenty overs with the new ball, and finished with career-best figures of 8-78 as the tourists were dismissed for 151.

Windows had made his County debut at the Cheltenham Festival aged just seventeen. He subsequently went up to Cambridge and won three cricket blues and a fives half-blue. After coming down, he had a promising first full season of County cricket, scoring over 600 Championship runs and taking 46 wickets to win his County cap.

He turned in several useful performances with bat and ball in 1966, but then in 1967 he decided to concentrate on his law studies and, for the next few years, he made only occasional appearances during his summer holidays. In 1974, he made a dramatic return to the side for their Sunday League match against Sussex at Moreton-in-Marsh and, despite not having played at County level for five years, he smashed a quick-fire 32, with four crisply-timed boundaries.

His son, Matthew, inherited Tony's prowess at ball and racquet sports, and the punchy young batsman has become the latest in a long line of pupils from Clifton College to win both a regular place in the Gloucestershire side, and honours with various England teams.

Matt Windows had a fine record at Clifton College, before reading Sociology at Durham University and winning a place in the Combined Universities team. In 1992, he followed in his

Matthew Guy Newman Windows
RHB, 1992-present

Born: 5 April 1973, Bristol

Batting

M	I	NO	Runs	Av
105	186	14	5928	34.47
134	126	13	2722	24.09

50	100	ct/st
30	13	61
9	2	41

Bowling

Balls	Runs	Wkts	Av	5wI	10wM
60	68	0	-	-	-
48	49	0			

Best Performances
184 v Warwickshire at Cheltenham, 1996
117 v Northamptonshire at Cheltenham, 2001

father's footsteps by making his Gloucestershire debut, and he also appeared for the England Under-19 side against their counterparts from Sri Lanka.

Initially, Windows appeared to be more of a workmanlike batsman with a solid technique, rather than a dashing stroke-maker. These characteristics saw him open the innings for a while, but in 1998 he moved back into the middle order and he has subsequently developed into a fluent run-maker. Like other short batsmen, the stocky Windows is particularly effective off the back foot, and, as befits a fine racquets player, he has a particularly powerful and wristy square-cut.

His maiden Championship hundred came against Warwickshire at Cheltenham in 1996, but only after he had been called back after initially appearing to be run out when in the eighties. However, umpire Dickie Bird, after consulting with his colleague Barrie Leadbeater, decided that visiting 'keeper Michael Burns had taken two attempts to remove the bails, and by the time they were dislodged, Windows had made his ground. To the relief of the Gloucestershire faithful, Bird recalled Windows, who reached his personal landmark a few overs later. In fact, he nearly went on to convert it into a double hundred, before being dismissed by Shaun Pollock for a fine 184.

Like several of the players on the County's staff, Windows has made rapid strides forward in the past few years under Mark Alleyne's leadership and the coaching of John Bracewell. In 1998, Matt Windows was Gloucestershire's Player of the Year, and their first batsman to score a thousand, finishing the summer with a Championship aggregate of 1,083 runs, and crowning a fine year by winning his County cap.

His move back into the middle order was at the behest of Bracewell, who felt Windows would be more comfortable lower down. Matt confirmed the views of the astute coach, hitting centuries against Yorkshire, Derbyshire, Kent and Essex, and winning a place in the England A squad for the winter tour to Zimbabwe and South Africa. Windows enjoyed a solid tour, hitting a pair of composed half-centuries in the match against the Zimbabwe President's XI, and he consolidated on these experiences the following summer when, for the second year running, he topped Gloucester-shire's batting averages.

The highlights of 1999 were a century against Essex at Gloucester, plus an unbeaten hundred off the Kent attack at Canter-bury, as well as being part of the County's side that won the NatWest Trophy and Benson & Hedges Super Cup. The following summer, he compiled a mature half-century in the B & H Cup Final, and helped the County to two more limited-overs titles. With the selectors rebuilding their squad in readiness for the 2003 World Cup, they could do far worse than looking at 'Steamy' Windows.

Born: 9 July 1858, Gloucester
Died: 4 April 1937, Montpellier, Cheltenham

Batting

M	I	NO	Runs	Av
140	224	53	1114	6.51
50	100	ct/st		
-	-	105		

Bowling

Balls	Runs	Wkts	Av	5wI	10wM
31414	11843	644	18.38	57	9

Best Performances
35 v Middlesex at Lord's
8-70 v Lancashire at Clifton

Billy Woof gave years of service to Gloucestershire cricket, initially as the club's second full-time professional, and then after twenty-three seasons with the County, he coached for many years at Cheltenham College, grooming a host of budding County players.

On leaving school, Woof had initially planned to train as an engineer, but he showed much promise as a left-arm seamer and played for the Gloucestershire Colts in 1878. A few words of encouragement from W.G. led Billy to rethink his career options and he decided to become a professional cricketer.

After a promising performance against a Gloucestershire XI at Cirencester, W.G. called up Woof for their Championship match against Sussex at Hove. However, Woof met with little immediate success, and without the guarantee of an engagement with Gloucestershire for the following summer, he accepted an offer from A.N. Hornby to spend 1879 on the groundstaff at Old Trafford.

Whilst attached to the Lancashire club, he cut back on his pace and concentrated instead on cut and spin. He met with greater success, and after watching him in the nets, Grace offered him a contract with Gloucestershire and arranged a post for him as the professional bowler at Cheltenham College.

For 1880, and for the next few years, Woof undertook the bulk of the bowling with W.G and Billy Midwinter. The clever left-armer soon met with success in his new style, and in 1884 he claimed 116 wickets in all games. This was followed by a haul of 100 wickets at barely 18 apiece in 1885, and his efforts helped the County to six wins from their fourteen matches. Amongst his excellent returns in 1885 were match figures of 12-134 against Surrey at The Oval , 12-50 in the innings victory over Somerset at Moreton-in-Marsh, and 11-114 in the return match at Taunton.

Between 1882 and 1885, Woof also had a place on the MCC groundstaff. In his first summer at Lord's, Woof took 6-14 against Kent, and then in the MCC's match against Nottinghamshire, Woof and Rylott sent down 64 balls at the start of the County's first innings without a run being scored from the bat, during which time six wickets fell.

In 1886, Billy Woof became cricket coach at Cheltenham College. This restricted his County appearances in the first part of the season, but Woof was back in the Gloucestershire side when the 1886 Australians played at the College during the Festival week and, to the delight of the watching schoolboys, he returned match figures of 9-76.

Woof only played infrequently from 1894 as other spinners came to the fore, and after his final match in 1902 he retired with a haul of 644 wickets for the County. For a while, Woof was also a first-class umpire, but he remained coach at Cheltenham College, helping to nurture several generations of promising young players.

Harry Wrathall
RHB & RM, 1894-1907

Born: 1 February 1869, Cheltenham
Died: 1 June 1944, Salisbury, Wiltshire

Batting

M	I	NO	Runs	Av
263	465	18	10284	23.00
50	**100**	**ct/st**		
46	8	180/3		

Bowling

Balls	Runs	Wkts	Av	5wI	10wM
1879	1288	27	47.70	-	-

Best Performances
176 v Somerset at Taunton, 1901
4-37 v Sussex at Hove, 1900

Harry Wrathall was a steady opening batsman, who in his early years had a reputation as being a stone-walling batsman. He subsequently belied this dour reputation, as in the course of his Gloucestershire career he amassed 10,284 runs, and passed a thousand runs on four occasions during his fourteen years of County cricket.

The Cheltenham-born opener made his first-class debut in 1894, but he had a fairly modest start, averaging just 8 in his 15 innings, and was described by *Wisden*'s correspondent as being 'scarcely up to County form'. However, W.G. had great faith in Wrathall's abilities, and he confirmed the doctor's opinion with 512 runs the following year, before moving up the order to open with W.G. in 1896.

He rather lived in the shadow of W.G., and did not at first enjoy opening with Grace. After losing confidence in 1897, he dropped back down the order, and continued to give often all too brief glimpses of batting talents. He also shared in two quite bizarre tail-end partnerships – firstly at Edgbaston in 1898, where he added 156 in ninety minutes with W.S.A.Brown for the ninth wicket against Warwickshire. Then, the following year, Wrathall added 106 with wicketkeeper Jack Board for the tenth wicket against Surrey at The Oval.

Wrathall moved back up the order to open following the departure in 1899 of W.G from the club and the responsibility this placed on him proved to be a major turning point in Wrathall's career. His maiden hundred, against Somerset at

Gloucester in June 1899, gave a huge boost to his confidence, and the following year he passed a thousand runs for the first time in his career.

Over the next few years, he went from strength to strength to become a far more fluent and harder hitting batsman, as well as the County's most dependable batsman after Gilbert Jessop. In August 1901, he struck a career best 176 against Somerset at Taunton in the space of just two and a half hours, with his innings containing no fewer than 32 boundaries. He finished the season with 1,450 runs to his name, and besides his century at Taunton, he made 135 against Sussex at Hove, plus innings at Bristol of 120 against Worcestershire and 125* against Surrey.

In 1903, he also shared an opening partnership of 277 with Theodore Fowler against London County at Crystal Palace. After leaving Gloucestershire in 1907, he played as a professional in Northumberland, and later in South Wales, where after the First World War, he was still one of the most successful professional batsmen in league cricket. Had he been in his thirties, rather than his fifties, Glamorgan might have used his services as they entered the County Championship in 1921.

Anthony John Wright

RHB, 1982-1998

Born: 27 June 1962, Stevenage, Hertfordshire

Batting

M	I	NO	Runs	Av
287	504	38	13440	28.84
278	261	21	6886	28.69
50	**100**	**ct/st**		
67	18	218		
44	4	94		

Bowling

Balls	Runs	Wkts	Av	5wI	10wM
74	68	1	68.00	-	-
26	22	0	-		

Best Performances

193 v Nottinghamshire at Bristol, 1995
1-16 v Yorkshire at Harrogate, 1989
177 v Scotland at Bristol, 1997

'Billy' Wright was a solid and most technically correct opening batsman, who with Dean Hodgson established a club record first-wicket stand of 362 against Nottinghamshire at Bristol in 1995. This was a worthy reward for the dependable batsman who earlier in his career had experienced several lows and a trough of despair when leading the county during a quite difficult transitional period in the early 1990s. A loss of form weighed on his mind – so much so, that he asked to stand down as captain – and it speaks volumes for Wright's steely determination and durability that he put these disappointments behind him and re-established his place at the top of the county's batting order.

Wright made his first-class debut in 1982 and, in 1987, he passed a thousand for the first time. In 1990, Wright was promoted to the captaincy and he teamed up with the county's new coach, Eddie Barlow. It proved to be a difficult time for both parties as the side suffered from injuries, lost valuable time due to bad weather and saw several players lose form. At the end of the season, Kevin Curran left the club, while Phil Bainbridge and David Graveney retired. The loss of three such experienced players left a hole in the county's resources for 1991, but Wright was able to oversee a promising first half to the season. Then, in 1992, he had Courtney Walsh back to spearhead the attack.

But just when things seemed to be on the up, both for Wright and Gloucestershire, events took a turn for the worse. Firstly, Eddie Barlow decided not to return for the final year of his contract, and then, in mid-season, Wright broke his hand. The following year, Wright lost form and confidence completely, dropped down from opening and then, with barely a couple of hundred runs to his name, asked to stand down from the captaincy in order to regain his touch.

To his credit, the following year he conquered the psychological demons that had tormented him, and he ended the 1994 season on top of the club's batting averages with over 1,100 Championship runs to his name. He met with even more success in 1995, amassing over 1,300 Championship runs, with the highlight of a vintage season being the record opening partnership of 362 in six hours against Nottinghamshire with Dean Hodgson.

In 1998, he also shared in a record partnership of 207 with Jack Russell in 1998, in their Benson & Hedges Cup tie with the British Universities. Their stand for the fourth wicket was a competition best, although it was not enough to prevent the students from winning the contest. Wright retired at the end of the summer and has subsequently acted as Second XI captain and coach, helping to groom the next generation of Gloucestershire cricketers.

Douglas Martin Young
RHB, 1949-1964

Born: 15 April 1924, Coalville, Leicestershire
Died: 18 June 1993, Pinelands, Cape Town

Batting

M	I	NO	Runs	Av
435	777	35	23400	31.53
2	2	0	22	11.00

50	100	ct/st
111	40	158
-	-	1

Bowling

Balls	Runs	Wkts	Av	5wI	10wM
170	130	3	43.33	-	-

Best Performances
198 v Oxford University at The Parks, 1962
2-35 v Surrey at The Oval, 1965
21 v Surrey at The Oval, 1964

Martin Young was very much a gentleman cricketer – educated at Wellingborough School, his off drives were as immaculate as his dapper dress sense. Together with his pukkah accent and smart appearance, he cut a most sophisticated figure off the field, and was very much an old smoothie.

On the field, his batting was assertive, but Young never took too many risks. A few critics suggested that he did not like short-pitched bowling but, at Bristol in 1963, he dispelled this with an assured and accomplished 127 against the fiery West Indian attack, as Gloucestershire chased a target of 280. The fact that they got within 66 runs of their target was entirely due to Young, who was first in and ninth out, after confidently driving, cutting and pulling the Caribbean attack for a memorable hundred. The next highest score in the Gloucestershire innings was John Mortimore's 26, and Young's scintillating efforts won fulsome praise from Frank Worrell, the West Indian captain, who after the match echoed the thoughts of many Gloucestershire supporters by asking 'Why isn't Young in the England side?'

Martin Young had joined Gloucestershire in 1949 after a brief spell on the Worcestershire staff. The first of his forty first-class centuries came the following year, against his former employers, and in this, his first full season of Championship cricket, he scored 1,558 runs. The short and sturdy man subsequently developed into a consistent and reliable opening batsman, with a steady temperament, solid technique and a wide array of classical strokes, especially through the offside. He formed a fine opening partnership with Ron Nicholls, and in 1962 the pair established a record opening partnership for Gloucestershire, adding 395 against Oxford University.

In 1955 and 1959, Young passed the two thousand run mark, and was part of a highly productive opening partnership with Arthur Milton.

One of his finest ever innings came in the match in 1959 with Northamptonshire at Bristol, as Gloucestershire chased 193 on the final afternoon. None of his colleagues were really at ease with the visiting attack, but Young batted with great assurance and skill to make a match-winning 108* to steer Gloucestershire home by two wickets.

Like many players, he had his own quirky mannerisms and always he kissed his bat before walking out to the wicket. He had every reason to show his gratitude, as his name was often touted as an England opener. But international honours never came his way, and he remained one of the most attractive and dependable opening batsmen on the County circuit, unlucky to be playing at a time when England were well blessed with many fine opening batsmen. He retired at the end of 1964 and emigrated to South Africa. Throughout his career, he had travelled there to coach during the winter months, and after retiring, he became a journalist and broadcaster with SABC.

Syed Zaheer Abbas

RHB & OB, 1972-1985

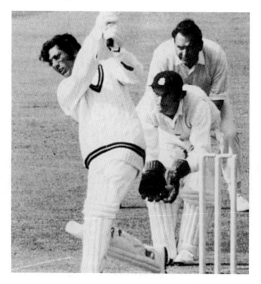

Born: 24 July 1947, Sialkot, Pakistan

Batting

M	I	NO	Runs	Av
206	360	37	16083	49.79
208	201	24	7098	40.10

50	100	ct/st
76	49	91
47	11	36

Bowling

Balls	Runs	Wkts	Av	5wl	10wM
669	332	6	55.33	-	-
165	114	4	28.50		

Best Performances

230* v Kent at Canterbury, 1976
3-32 v Warwickshire at Gloucester, 1981
129* v Middlesex at Lord's, 1981
1-11 v Yorkshire at Cheltenham, 1983

Zaheer Abbas was a stylish and fluent stroke-maker, whose prolific batting record led to him being dubbed the 'Asian Bradman'. He burst onto the world stage in the early 1970s after equalling Hanif Mohammad's record of five centuries in six innings in domestic cricket in Pakistan, and winning a place on their tour to England in 1971. In only his second Test appearance, the bespectacled youngster hit a double century at Edgbaston. So solid was his concentration that at one stage it looked as if the gifted Pakistani would make a triple hundred, but after over nine hours at the crease, he eventually fell for 274.

This fine innings led to offers from several counties, but after a glowing recommendation from Sadiq, Gloucestershire was Zaheer's choice. During a loyal association with the County, 'Zed' played a host of cultured innings, full of majestic and silky smooth stroke-play, with the ball being almost effortlessly despatched to the boundary on both sides of the wicket. An innings from this prince of batsmen was certainly a treasure to behold, unless of course, you happened to be a member of the opposition attack!

Zaheer's success was built on a quick eye, razor-sharp reflexes, supple wrists, a high back-lift, a rock-solid temperament, and a desire to mercilessly dominate the bowlers. He belied his mild disposition off the field by being quite ruthless on it, and time and time again, Zaheer was quite awesome in his single-handed dissection of all kinds of bowling, scoring with such finesse and regularity off even good-length balls. Of his contemporaries in County cricket, perhaps only the two Richards – Barry and Viv – stood ahead of him, and in the mid-1970s 'Zed' would have been an automatic choice in any World XI.

Only on the very fastest and bounciest of wickets did Zaheer ever look uneasy at the crease. It was a completely different matter however on the more green and gentle wickets of England and, to the delight of Gloucestershire folk, the modest and softly-spoken Pakistani devoured the most potent of county attacks. 1976 and 1981 were his most successful summers for Gloucestershire, during which he passed two thousand runs in first-class games.

1976 also saw him top the national batting averages, and all after despatching the Surrey attack for 216* and 156* at The Oval, followed by scores of 230* and 104* against Kent at Canterbury. The following year at Cheltenham he repeated the feat of a double hundred and a century, all unbeaten in the same match, with 205* and 108* against Sussex at Cheltenham, and then in 1981 he made 215* and 150* against Somerset at Bath. Such run-scoring sprees delighted the Gloucestershire fans, but his liking for playing long innings did, however, place quite a strain on his lean frame, and in order to build up his stamina, 'Zed' would gleefully consume porridge and Guinness!